When Good Things Happen to Bad People:

Fifty Case Studies of Notorious Villains

By Martin H. Levinson

iUniverse, Inc.
New York   Bloomington

When Good Things Happen to Bad People
Fifty Case Studies of Notorious Villains

iUniverse books may be ordered through booksellers or by contacting:

iUniverse
1663 Liberty Drive
Bloomington, IN 47403
www.iuniverse.com
1-800-Authors (1-800-288-4677)

ISBN: 978-1-4401-2012-1 (pbk)
ISBN: 978-1-4401-2013-8 (ebk)

Printed in the United States of America

iUniverse rev. date: 1/30/2009

To Katherine Liepe-Levinson
A very, very good person

TABLE OF CONTENTS

INTRODUCTION

When Good Things Happen to Bad People offers an irreverent, fast-paced, fact-filled compendium of fifty case studies of notorious villains from Attila the Hun to Dick Cheney who triumphed in life despite, or because of, their dastardly deeds. This book is the perfect foil to Harold Kushner's international bestseller *When Bad Things Happen to Good People*.

Strictly speaking, there is no scientific way to determine whether someone is or is not a "bad person." But I suspect most of us would agree that individuals who commit atrocities or who consistently cause harm toward others for self-serving reasons deserve the label "bad people."

So why do good things happen to bad people? Maybe a certain number of baddies are simply going to get their share of good luck. Maybe "the devil" is running the universe and he or she likes pleasing his or her favorites. Maybe God is playing a joke on bad people by rewarding them on earth and then punishing them in an afterlife. Or maybe Edmund Burke was on the right track when he said, "All that is necessary for the triumph of evil is that good men do nothing." For evil to triumph less, it follows that good people need to do something—like exposing wickedness when they are confronted with it. As the saying goes: "Sunshine is the best disinfectant."

NERO (37-68)

Nero, the fifth and last Roman emperor of the Julio-Claudian dynasty, had a rule characterized by tyranny and waste. He executed lots of people, including his mother and adoptive brother, purportedly "fiddled" while Rome burned, and persecuted the Christians to such an extent that the church labeled him the first antichrist. Nero was not exactly a chamber-of-commerce type guy.

Nero killed his mother, Agrippina, because he was angry that she objected to an affair he was having. To bring about her death he made various attempts on her life, three of which were by poison and one by rigging the ceiling over her bed to collapse while she lay in it. When these actions failed he enticed Agrippina into a leaky boat, which was intended to sink in the Bay of Naples. Sadly for him, she managed to swim ashore. Exasperated, Nero dispatched an assassin who clubbed and stabbed the poor woman to death.

As far as fiddling while Rome burned, it is uncertain who, or what, started the Great Fire of Rome in July 64. But Tacitus says the population searched for a fall guy and rumor held Nero responsible—it was said that he played his lyre and sang while the city was combusting around him. To deflect blame, Nero targeted the Christians, ordering a number to be fed to the lions, while others were crucified and set ablaze—some at night, providing illumination for his private grounds. This scapegoat strategy appeased the masses and allowed Nero to continue in his wicked ways.

Nero had a liking for excess. He kicked his wife to death when she griped about his returning home late from the races, he won contests he did not train for in the Olympic Games—such as winning the chariot race while falling

1

off his chariot (nobody dared to defeat him), he took part in wild orgies, and he forced people to stay in the auditorium when he was performing (one woman gave birth during one of his concerts and there are stories of men who pretended to die so they could be carried out). Nero believed, like a popular beer commercial of a few years ago, that you only go around once in life, so you should grab all the gusto you can.

Toward the end of his reign, an increase in the execution of senators, noblemen, and generals, and a serious food shortage led to an insurrection. Nero's troops joined the rebellion, as did members of the Roman Senate who voted that the emperor be flogged to death. He chose to commit suicide and die on his own terms instead. His last words were, "Jupiter, what an artist the world loses in me!" Though he was only 31 when he departed this mortal coil, Nero had had one heck of a ride.

Tacitus writes that many in the upper classes welcomed Nero's death. But members of the lower classes, slaves, patrons of the arena and the theater, and "those who were supported by the famous excesses of Nero" were upset with the news. They had great affection for their madcap monarch and missed not having him around, which proves something all successful politicians know: if you want the public to like you give them loads of bread and circuses.

ATTILA THE HUN (406-453)

People with sadistic tendencies usually rein in their malicious impulses so they don't wind up ostracized or in jail. That was not the case for Attila the Hun. He acted on his brutal inclinations and through them gained recognition and riches. What a lucky Hun!

Attila and his brother, Bleda, succeeded their uncle as co-leaders of the Huns in 434. Then Bleda conveniently died—killed by Attila say the classical sources—and Attila became the leader of the Hunnic Empire, which stretched from Germany to the Ural River and from the Danube River to the Baltic Sea. To this day in Western Europe, Attila is remembered as the embodiment of greed and cruelty. In Woody Allen's satirical 1975 film *Love and Death*, Diane Keaton's character argues a plan to assassinate Napoleon with this alleged quote by Attila: "Violence is justified in the service of mankind."

In 441, Attila invaded the Eastern Roman Empire, the success of which prompted him to invade the West. He passed unimpeded through Austria and Germany, across the Rhine and into Gaul (modern France), looting and destroying all in his path with a crazed viciousness unmatched in the annals of barbarian invasions. He was called the "Scourge of God" because of his propensity to pillage and plunder with carefree abandon. In 452, Attila's army completely razed the city of Aquileia—legend has it he built a castle on top of a hill north of the town just to watch it burn.

Although Attila was a wealthy thug, he was not a flamboyant one. He wore plain clothes, eschewing attire with any sort of ornamentation. In the tradition of Mongol warriors, he also ingested mare's milk, blood, and raw meat when necessary. But Attila had a penchant for the ladies and he possessed a number of wives. (St. Ursula was not one of them. When she turned down his wedding proposal he killed her with an arrow and had 11,000 of her followers massacred.) This weakness for female companionship eventually did him in.

Attila died in 453, on the night of one of his marriages, after drinking an excessive amount of alcohol to celebrate a new bride. His end wasn't pretty. He passed out flat on his back, had a massive nosebleed, and choked on his own blood. Outside of his own clan, many people concluded that a good thing had happened to a bad person.

In 1990, Attila was resurrected in a runaway bestseller titled *Leadership Secrets of Attila the Hun*. The book draws on Attila's imaginary thoughts and "reveals his principles for successful morale building, decision making, delegating and negotiating, and gives advice on overcoming setbacks and achieving goals." In 1994, a follow-up volume titled *Victory Secrets of Attila the Hun*, which looks to Attila and the history of the Roman Empire for effective business strategies, was also published. While the Scourge of God may no longer be with us, his barbarian philosophy clearly lives on.

GENGHIS KHAN (1165-1227)

Genghis Khan, the founder and ruler of the Mongol Empire, seized or overran more territory than any other conqueror in history. During his lifetime the Mongol Empire occupied most of Asia. Genghis was a man with a plan, and that plan was world domination.

Genghis was a natural-born killer and he started his killing young, at age 13, with the murder of his half-brother Bekhter, whom he slew with an arrow in a dispute over sharing hunting spoils. Although his mother scolded him harshly for slaying his sibling, Genghis never expressed any remorse. The incident locked in his position as head of the household and led his remaining brothers to think twice about quarrelling with their bad-tempered kinsman.

In his youth, Genghis was captured in a raid and imprisoned by a tribe that put him in a cangue (a device similar to the stocks that are used for punishment in the West). Luckily for him, he was able to escape his restraints with the help of a sympathetic guard and hide in a river crevice. The breakout enhanced his reputation as a tough guy and helped him to recruit a couple of his future generals who, along with his brothers, provided soldiers for early expansion.

Genghis was an expert at dealing out death and destruction. For example, when attacking Volohoi (a walled city in Tibet), Genghis convinced the city commander that the Mongols would stop their aggression if the city sent out 1,000 cats and several thousand swallows. When he got them, Genghis had bits of cloth tied to their tails and the material was set ablaze. The cats and birds fled back to Volohoi and ended up starting many fires inside. Then

Genghis attacked and slaughtered the town's inhabitants. Another time, the Mongols rounded up 70,000 men, women, and children and shot them with arrows.

Genghis once told his comrades: "Man's greatest good fortune is to chase and defeat his enemy, seize his total possessions, leave his married women weeping and wailing, ride his gelding, use his women as a nightshirt and support, gazing upon and kissing their rosy breasts, sucking their lips which are as sweet as the berries of their breasts." That's a statement worthy of Attila the Hun.

In Iraq, Iran, Afghanistan, Russia, Ukraine, Poland, and Hungary, Genghis is looked upon as a vicious and genocidal warlord who caused enormous damage and destruction. However, he has been venerated for centuries among the Mongols (his name and likeness can be found on products, streets, buildings, and other places, and his face is on the largest denominations of Mongolian currency), who claim that the history written by non-Mongolians has been unduly biased against Genghis and that his cruelty has been exaggerated. And in much of modern-day Turkey it has become popular for male children to carry Genghis' title in their names. As is often the case in history, no matter how brutal a despot is, if he acquires land for people, they will think highly of him.

Tomás de Torquemeda (1420-1498)

After working for a while as a commonplace monk and monastery cook, Tomás de Torquemada gained the acquaintance of Spanish King Ferdinand and Queen Isabella. As a result he was appointed Inquisitor General in 1483, and for the next fifteen years he oversaw the Spanish Inquisition, which was established in 1478 by Ferdinand and Isabella as a way to unify the country by maintaining Catholic orthodoxy in Spain.

The Inquisition was characterized by a viciousness and evil efficiency scarcely equaled before the twentieth century. Its practices included torture, anonymous denunciation, and handing over convicted heretics to secular authorities for execution by fire, which was performed as a public spectacle labeled an *auto-da-fé*. If the condemned recanted and kissed the cross, they were mercifully strangled before the fire was set. If they recanted only, they were set ablaze with a quick-burning seasoned wood. If they did not recant, they were roasted with slow-burning green wood.

Every Christian over the age of twelve (for girls) and fourteen (for boys) was answerable to the Inquisition. Heretics, particularly those who had converted to Christianity from Judaism to avoid expulsion from Spain, were the main targets but anyone who spoke against the Inquisition was fair game.

To help resist the spread of heresy, Torquemada encouraged the burning of non-Catholic literature, especially Jewish Talmuds. Arabic books were burnt as well after the final defeat of the Moors at Granada in 1492. That same year Torquemada also endorsed the Alhambra decree, which resulted in the mass expulsion of Jews from Spain. He wisely kept quiet about the fact that his grandmother was a *conversa,* a converted Jew.

Many people, including Pope Sixtus IV, complained about Inquisition excesses. The pope noted: "The Inquisitors at Seville, without observing juridical prescriptions, have detained many persons in violation of justice, punishing them by severe tortures and imputing to them, without foundation, the crime of heresy, and despoiling of their wealth those sentenced to death, in such form that a great number of them have come to the Apostolic See, fleeing from such excessive rigor and protesting their orthodoxy." To ease the pope's concerns, and to stay on in the Inquisition business, Torquemada dispatched his representative to Rome on three separate occasions to defend his ruthless actions.

In the last years of his life, Torquemada was convinced that he would be poisoned and he kept a unicorn's horn by his plate as an antidote. However, he never had to use that remedy. He died of natural causes at the ripe old age of 78. But while the man may have expired, his evil work lived on, eviscerating new victims long after he was gone. (Statistics show that between 1471 and 1781, Spain was drained of free thinkers at the rate of 1,000 per annum.) The "hammer of heretics" even in death just kept on hammering.

VLAD THE IMPALER (1431-1476)

Vlad the Impaler, aka Vladislav Dracula or simply Dracula, was a prince of Wallachia, a former kingdom that is now part of Romania. Known for the tremendously cruel punishments that he imposed during his reign, Vlad is also famous for having a celebrated literary figure named after him, the vampire main character in Bram Stoker's 1897 novel, *Dracula.*

When Vlad and his brother were young, their father, a Wallachian ruler, gave them over to the Sultan of the Ottoman Empire as a gesture of goodwill to prevent a Turkish invasion. This transfer did not sit well with Vlad and he behaved in a stubborn and rude manner, which led the Sultan to frequently whip him. But when the Turks invaded Wallachia the Sultan decided to let bygones be bygones, and in 1447 he installed Vlad on the throne as a puppet ruler (Vlad's father had been murdered by *boyars*, high-ranking feudal Wallachians, so he was not available for the job).

Vlad's rule was short, as Hunyadi, the regent of Hungary, marched into Wallachia and ousted him the same year. Vlad fled to Moldavia and after that he went to Hungary, where he impressed Hunyadi with his knowledge of the behind-the-scenes workings of the Ottoman Empire as well as his hatred of the Sultan. Suitably swayed, Hunyadi pardoned Vlad, made him his advisor, and smoothed the way for him to become the ruler of Wallachia, a place that he governed with an iron fist, or to be more precise, an iron spear.

Vlad made his points through impalement. One of his favorite methods of torture was to have a horse attached to each of the victim's legs as a honed and well-oiled stake was slowly put into the anus and forced through the individual until it came out from their mouth. Sometimes victims were impaled through other bodily openings or through the abdomen or chest. Infants were occasionally impaled on a stake forced through their mother's torso. Some victims were impaled so that they hung upside down on the stake.

While impalement was Vlad's preferred means of torture, it was by no means his only one. The tortures he employed were wide-ranging: nails in heads, cutting off limbs, blinding, strangulation, burning, cutting off noses and ears, mutilation of sexual organs, scalping, skinning, exposure to the elements or to animals, and boiling alive. According to an old Romanian folktale, one day Vlad left a gold cup in the middle of a road. He retrieved it the next day, as no one had taken it; people were terrified to do anything improper due to the horrific torments that could be inflicted on them.

Among the Romanian peasantry today, Vlad is not remembered as a sadistic, homicidal fanatic, but rather as a just prince who defended his people from foreign aggression. He is also fondly thought of as a champion of the common man against the oppression of the boyars. And it is not just the hayseeds who venerate the Vlad. Romanian presidential candidate Traian Basescu referred to the Impaler and his way of punishing recalcitrant behavior in an anticorruption speech that he gave during his election campaign in 2004. Unlike Vladislav Dracula, who was able to skewer his opposition in the flesh, today's Romanian leaders can only symbolically stick it to those who oppose them.

POPE ALEXANDER VI (1431-1503)

Pope Alexander VI (Rodrigo Borgia) was one of the most corrupt popes in history. Fourteen years after his death, the papal dissipation that Alexander VI epitomized would prompt a young monk named Martin Luther to nail a summary of his grievances on the door of a church in Germany and launch the Protestant Reformation. Alexander's surname has become a catchphrase for Rome's depraved standards during the Renaissance era.

Rodrigo was fortunate in choosing his relatives. When he was twenty-five, and not even a priest, his uncle, Pope Calixtus III, conferred the red hat of a cardinal onto his nephew. A year later the lad was made head of the entire Curia, the administrative branch of the Holy See.

When Pope Innocent VIII died in 1492, the bribes offered by Cardinal Borgia to his friendly colleagues were sufficient to guarantee his election as pope by a bare two-thirds majority. Giovanni di Lorenzo de Medici, who would later become Pope Leo X, said of Borgia's selection, "Now we are in the power of a wolf, the most rapacious perhaps that this world has ever seen. And if we do not flee, he will inevitably devour us all." Alexander certainly had a voracious appetite.

Pope Alexander's two main obsessions were greed for gold and love of women, and he pursued both passions with great zeal. He was especially devoted to the children his girlfriends bore him, a dedication that may have included an incestuous relationship with his daughter, Lucrezia. For his offspring he was prepared to commit any transgression and thrust all the

Italian states into war. He gave his kids the material resources of the Church as if he personally owned them.

Alexander constantly needed money and to get it, he sold church offices to the highest bidders and kept open vacancies caused by the deaths of bishops and cardinals so the papacy could collect the wealth that streamed in from their offices. He dispensed indulgences (written proclamations that absolved individuals from punishment in the afterlife for sins that had been committed in this one) like a first-rate entrepreneur: If you wanted one you could get one, if you had the dough. He also sold divorce decrees. (In 1529, King Henry VIII declared himself head of the English Church, breaking his allegiance to Rome, so that he might obtain a divorce from his first wife, Catherine of Aragon. Had Alexander been pope at the time, Henry probably would have gotten his divorce and England would have remained Catholic.)

One positive aspect of Alexander's life was his appreciation and patronage of the arts—Raphael, Michelangelo, Bramante, Pinturicchio, and many other Renaissance notables worked for him. Though love and support of culture may not balance the fact that during Alexander's pontificate the church was brought to its lowest level of degradation, it shows that the man wasn't completely appalling.

FRANCISCO PIZARRO (CA. 1471-1541)

Francisco Pizarro was a Spanish conquistador who conquered the largest amount of territory ever taken in a single battle when he defeated the Incan Empire at Cajamarca, a city in Peru, in 1532. Pizarro's victory opened the way for Spain to claim most of South America and its vast riches, as well as to imprint the continent with Spanish culture, language, and religion.

The son of a soldier and a common maid, Pizarro received little if any formal education as a child, but he was clever and ambitious and instinctively understood both power and politics. It was through such understanding that he was able to convince Charles V of Spain to grant him an official coat of arms, the brand new rank of captain general, and the governorship of all lands more than six hundred miles south of Panama. With these perks in place, on December 27, 1530, Pizarro led an expedition that set sail from Panama for Peru.

After arriving at the Peruvian coast, Pizarro headed for the center of the Incan Empire with a force of 167 conquistadors, to fight an Incan army of perhaps eighty thousand warriors. He not only met the enemy, he annihilated it, as he was able to employ sixteenth-century European military technology—horses, steel helmets, armor, and chain mail—against wooden clubs and bows and arrows.

In his Peruvian campaign, Pizarro first captured Atahualpa, the revered Inca emperor. Then he marched into Cuzco, the Incan capital, and took it.

He held Atahualpa as a hostage but ultimately executed him, despite being paid a king's ransom of one room filled with gold and two with silver, which was later split among Pizarro's closest associates.

The execution of Atahualpa, by most accounts a lovely fellow whom his people considered a God-like figure, established a model that the Spanish later followed. All Incan rulers became targets for abuse, as did members of their families. Francisco's brother, Gonzalo, seized the wife of Atahualpa's successor and kept her as his own.

Despite pleas to Pizarro from some in Spain for better treatment of the natives, he and his conquistadors slaughtered countless numbers of innocent civilians and poorly armed soldiers. They pillaged the wealth of the Inca Empire, murdered its leaders, and destroyed many of its architectural masterpieces. And they set up a system of Spanish control that to this day marginalizes indigenous Peruvians.

In 1535, Pizarro took up residence in Lima where he lived like a king for a number of years in an ornate palace. But in 1541, his good fortune ran out when followers of Pedro de Almagro (Cortes' captain), who wanted to seize the Peruvian capital for its riches, assassinated him.

While Pizarro may have gone to meet his maker, his fame still lives on through statues (there's one depicting him on horseback in Lima), literature, and films. Pizarro's latest popular allusion is in the 2007 movie *Pirates of the Caribbean: At World's End*. It occurs when Captain Jack Sparrow, speaking to a group of prostitutes, says, "By the way, no, I have never actually met Pizarro but I love his pies."

HENRY VIII (1491-1547)

Henry VIII was a ruthless regent who resolved many of his problems by having people executed. His friends and wives often wound up on the chopping block. Egotistical, greedy and mean, Henry was also a homophobe who introduced legislation against homosexuals with the Buggery Act, which made "buggery" punishable by hanging, a penalty not finally lifted until 1861. He is probably best known for his six marriages.

Catherine of Aragon, Henry's first wife, had six pregnancies over nine years but none produced a male heir. He used that excuse to dump her and when the Pope did not allow Henry to annul his marriage, he dumped the Holy Father and declared himself head of the English Church. By abolishing Catholicism, Henry was able to sell or enjoy the profits of England's Catholic monasteries. He got a twofer, so to speak—an opportunity to marry a new wife and lots of new riches. As the saying goes, "It's good to be king."

Wife number two, Anne Boleyn, *aka* Anne of the 1,000 Days because she reigned for only 1,000 days from 1533 to 1536, also did not bear a son. That was not a good move, as Henry had taken a fancy to Jane Seymour, one of Anne's ladies-in-waiting. To make a long story short, Anne was arrested on trumped-up charges, convicted of them, and beheaded.

Henry married Jane Seymour within 24 hours of Anne Boleyn's execution. Unlike the first two queens, Jane never had a coronation. But she did have a boy. Unfortunately for her, Jane expired just two weeks after the little fellow was born.

Anne of Cleves, whom he married for political gain, was Henry's fourth consort. However, he found her unattractive—it is said he called her a "Flanders Mare"—and she wasn't skilled at music and literature, which were popular at Henry's court. After six months the marriage was annulled.

Catherine Howard, a girl no more than nineteen years of age and wife number five, was less than a year into matrimony when rumors of her infidelity began. Evidence was quickly assembled that the Queen had been promiscuous before her nuptials and that she may have had liaisons afterwards. In 1542, Catherine Howard went the way of Anne Boleyn—executed on the Tower Green.

Henry's last spouse, Katherine Parr, was lucky that Henry passed away before anything too terrible could happen to her. But a year and a half after Henry's demise, Katherine's good fortune ran out when she died shortly after giving birth to a baby girl.

A narcissistic self-serving monarch, Henry VIII wanted it all: wealth, women, and worshipful devotion from all his subjects. He may not have realized that last goal but he certainly achieved the first two and, as Meat Loaf so eloquently put it in one of his hit rock songs, two out of three ain't bad.

Ivan the Terrible (1530-1584)

Ivan the Terrible was the first Russian head of state to bear the title *tsar*. His long term in office (41 years) saw the reform of the government, church, and army; the conquest of Siberia; and the establishment of Russia as a multiethnic state. But there's much more to the story.

As a young man Ivan was a psychopath and heavy imbiber of alcohol. He threw dogs and cats from the Kremlin walls and roamed Moscow's neighborhoods with a bunch of toughs, drinking, beating up seniors, and raping women. He frequently disposed of the ladies he assaulted by having them hanged, strangled, buried alive, or thrown to the bears.

On December 29, 1543, before he was crowned king, Ivan called his boyars (great nobles) to a meeting. He reprimanded them for their indifference to both him and the nation and said their leader, Prince Andrew Shuiksy, would have to be disciplined. Then, at a signal from Ivan, a group of armed huntsmen seized Shuiksy and forced him outside, where, in front of a multitude of mesmerized Muscovites, the petrified prince was thrown before a pack of ravenous hunting dogs that pounced upon the poor fellow and ate him.

In the 1560s, Ivan formed a secret police force known as the Oprichniki who were used as instruments of his rule. Many in the group were criminals. When Ivan founded a pseudo-monastic order, he had the Oprichniki regularly perform sacrilegious masses that included extended orgies of sex, rape, and torture. Ivan frequently acted as the master of ceremonies at these rituals.

In 1570, on the basis of unproved accusations of treason, Ivan sacked and burned the city of Novgorod and tortured, mutilated, stabbed, roasted, and otherwise slaughtered its citizens. Novgorod's archbishop was sewn up in a bearskin and then hunted to death by a bunch of hounds. Men, women, and children were lashed to sleighs, which were then run into the freezing waters of the Volkhov River. The mass of corpses caused the Volkhov to flood its banks.

In 1581, Ivan beat his pregnant daughter-in-law for wearing "brazen attire," which may have caused a miscarriage. When his son, also named Ivan, heard about this he got into a heated argument with his father, which resulted in Ivan hitting the boy in the head with his staff causing the lad's demise. This event is depicted in a well-known painting by Ilya Repin, *Ivan the Terrible and his son Ivan on 16 November, 1581*, better known as *Ivan the Terrible killing his son*.

Despite Ivan's extraordinary cruelty, his reign is considered a great one in Russian folk chronicles. His nickname in Russian is "Grozny," which has always been translated as "the Terrible," but actually means "the Awesome." For my money, I'd go with "the Terrible."

ELIZABETH BÁTHORY (1560-1614)

Elizabeth Báthory was a highly educated Hungarian countess and a sadistic serial killer of young girls. She pursued her murderous behavior for many years without official interference, but in 1609 Elizabeth decided to bump off a number of young women from aristocratic families without much wealth. The deaths of peasant girls might be disregarded, but the slaying of lasses from the upper classes had to be looked into.

The King of Hungary ordered Elizabeth's arrest and her cousin, Count Thurzó (the prime minister of Hungary), quickly stepped in to save the family from disgrace by arranging for her capture in the best way he thought possible. He ordered a raid on Elizabeth's house that seized four of her accomplices, three women and a man. Elizabeth was detained but not taken away.

In January 1611, three of the arrested collaborators were subjected to two trials and convicted of their awful misdeeds in a matter of days. The following are some descriptions of torture that emerged during the proceedings: (a) biting the flesh off faces, arms, and other body parts; (b) burning or disfiguring of hands, sometimes also of faces and genitalia; (c) severe beatings over extended periods of time, often with fatal outcomes; (d) freezing to death; (e) the use of needles; (e) starving of victims. On the plus side, there were no allegations of water boarding.

The two female defendants were sentenced to have their fingers, which had been "dipped in the blood of Christians," torn out with red-hot pincers, and then to be burned alive. The man was decapitated before his body was set ablaze alongside the two women. Elizabeth was not present at either trial and was not convicted of any wrongdoing.

When Elizabeth attempted to run away, Thurzó had her confined to her castle at Cachtice, where stonemasons walled up the windows and the door to Elizabeth's bedchamber with Elizabeth inside (as horrible as this seems, it beats what happened to her partners in crime). There she spent the remaining three years of her life, with only a small opening for food to be passed to her, before dying at age fifty-four, a fairly long life span considering that life expectancy in the 15th and 16th centuries was only about 30 to 40 years.

The number of young women tortured and killed by Elizabeth is unknown, but it is often cited as being in the hundreds. One witness who spoke at the trial told of a book in which a total of 650 victims was alleged to have been listed by Elizabeth. Whether this figure is true or not, Elizabeth Báthory certainly murdered and tortured enough people to justify the nickname that history has bestowed on her—the "Blood Countess."

MATTHEW HOPKINS

(UNKNOWN-1647)

Matthew Hopkins was an English witch hunter who was responsible for the killing of around 300 women in England between the years 1644 and 1646. Many of these women were accused of witchcraft by children and convicted on evidence such as third nipples (considered to be the mark of Satan); a boil, scar, or birthmark that would not bleed when perforated; or even owning a cat. Hopkins held the self-appointed office of "Witch-finder General," a title that was never bestowed by Parliament.

Not much is known about Hopkins' early life. He is thought to have been the son of a Puritan minister from Great Wenham. He became a solicitor, but attempts to begin a practice failed twice. He was attracted to his new trade after hearing some women talk about their meetings with the Devil. A light bulb went on in his demented skull as he realized witch-finding might be a good career move.

Torture was officially prohibited in England, so to expose witches Hopkins used a variety of "less coercive methods" to wrest confessions from his victims. For example, he used sleep deprivation to extort information. He also employed a "swimming test" to see if the accused would float in water, the theory being that water would preternaturally reject those who forsook baptism when entering the Devil's service. And he utilized "witch prickers" who stuck the accused with knives and special needles, looking for the Devil's stain that was supposed to be numb to all feeling and would not bleed.

Elizabeth Clarke of Manningtree was his first victim. She was coerced to give evidence that led Hopkins to five other women, one of whom directed him to still other innocents to save her own life. Ultimately, 32 women were accused of being witches and 28 of them were convicted in a trial that took place at Chelmsford. Four died in jail, and the rest were hanged.

Females weren't the only ones persecuted and prosecuted by the Witch-finder General. One of his targets was John Lowes, an 80-year-old vicar whose parishioners wanted him removed from office because he was a bit cantankerous. As Lowes had sided with a woman who had been convicted of witchcraft, the worshippers asked Hopkins to interrogate him. Hopkins did that and, using his customary techniques, he succeeded in having the vicar tried, sentenced and executed.

Local magistrates paid Hopkins quite well for his witch-hunting work, reimbursing him up to 20 shillings for each "witch" he exposed who was then found guilty of witchcraft (20 shillings represented about 19 weeks' salary for the average Englishman). Hopkins and his co-worker, John Stearne, once earned 20 pounds from a business trip to Stowmarket. Most folks in the 17th century would have had to labor for more than a year to make that much money.

Hopkins either died from tuberculosis or was hung (historians are divided on the point) in 1647. But his legacy as Britain's most notorious witch hunter lives on in songs, books, and films—the 1968 movie *Witchfinder General* has even developed a cult following. Unlike many people's fifteen minutes of fame, Hopkins' celebrity has kept on going.

Ranavalona I (1782-1861)

When King Radama I of Madagascar died in 1828 he left no direct descendants. According to local custom his rightful heir was Rakotobe, the oldest son of the king's eldest sister. However, Radama's wife, Ranavalona, found out about her husband's death before Rakotobe and she managed to secure the throne by imprisoning Rakotobe and other likely rivals. She then killed almost all of Radama's relatives, renounced the treaties he had negotiated with the British Empire, and legalized the slave trade. The woman who has been called the *Female Caligula* was on a roll.

To eradicate Christianity from her island, Ranavalona ordered the expulsion of all missionaries. When that plan failed to accomplish her goal, she decided to become a violent persecutor of the native Christians. All people who possessed a bible, or who claimed to be Christian, were condemned to die.

One of Ranavalona's favorite methods of killing people was to have a prisoner put in a pit at the bottom of a hill and have her soldiers, at the top of the hill, tip over pots of boiling water. When the liquid reached the floor of the pit it would gradually ascend and scald the prisoner to death. Another execution technique was to yoke people together like farm animals and place them in the thick matted jungles of Madagascar where they would break their necks trying to get free, or would get caught in the undergrowth and starve to death. A third practice involved dressing the victim in the bloody skins of animals and setting hunting dogs upon them.

To keep the royal coffers full, Ranavalona mounted predatory military expeditions against tribes not allied with her. Looting and pillaging, the queen's forces would attack their fellow Madagascarans, leaving a path of death and destruction in their wake. In these rapacious campaigns against her own people, Ranavalona showed she was one tough lady.

She was also one clever lady. For example, when Ranavalona found out that some local leaders and Europeans had hatched a conspiracy against her, she quickly snuffed the locals out. But she couldn't bump off the Europeans for fear of reprisals. Therefore she made their normally weeklong trip to the coast a particularly gruesome and lengthy one, lasting 53 days, so that they were utterly drained when they finally reached their departure point.

Ranavalona passed away peacefully in her sleep after a thirty-three-year reign in which at least a third of the inhabitants of Madagascar died on her orders, either executed or worked to death as forced labor. Some say her rule was good for Madagascar, as she kept foreign colonial powers from taking over the country. While there may be some truth in this, it is also true that if the monarchs who succeeded her had continued Ranavalona's brutal policies there would have been no one left to colonize.

WILLIAM TECUMSEH SHERMAN

(1820-1891)

William Tecumseh Sherman, the originator of the term "war is hell," was an American military leader, businessman, teacher and writer. Named after the famous Shawnee leader Tecumseh, Sherman decimated American Indian populations in the west after the Civil War. During the Civil War he gained great notoriety for his scorched-earth crusade through Georgia.

Before embarking on that venture, Sherman, a West Point graduate, served as the president of a San Francisco bank that failed. He also labored unsuccessfully as a lawyer in Leavenworth, Kansas. When the War Between the States began, he finally found work he could succeed at.

Sherman enlisted as an officer in the Union army, where he cultivated a friendship with General Ulysses S. Grant. He wrote to Grant outlining his strategy to bring the conflict to an end: "...if you can whip Lee and I can march to the Atlantic I think ol' Uncle Abe will give us twenty days leave to see the young folks." Sherman then proceeded to invade Georgia with three armies, capturing the city of Atlanta on September 2, 1864.

A little over a month later, Sherman severed the last telegraph wire that connected him to the military brass in the north and began his famous "March to the Sea." Nothing was heard from him for five weeks as his troops trudged from Atlanta towards Savannah, cutting a swath of death and desolation. Plantations were burned, crops were destroyed, and stores of food were pillaged. Women were gang-raped and thousands, including women and children of all races, were killed. Sherman's soldiers also left "Sherman sentinels" (chimneys of burnt-out houses) and "Sherman neckties" (railroad rails that had been heated and wrapped around trees) as souvenirs of their tramp through the Peach State. At the end of his ruinous campaign of "total warfare," Sherman's forces took Savannah.

After Lee surrendered at Appomattox, Sherman began a crusade of ethnic genocide against the Plains Indians: "The more Indians we can kill this year the fewer we will need to kill the next, because the more I see of the Indians the more convinced I become that they must either all be killed or be maintained as a species of pauper. Their attempts at civilization is [*sic*] ridiculous…"

Most of the raids on Indian camps were carried out during winter, when families were together and could therefore be murdered in one fell swoop. Sherman encouraged his soldiers to massacre men, women and children during the attacks. Livestock was also slaughtered so that any survivors would be more likely to starve to death. By 1890, the Plains Indians were either all dead or on reservations.

Sherman retired from the army in 1884 and was proposed as a Republican candidate for that year's presidential election. Twentieth-century tributes have included a gilded bronze equestrian statue at the entrance to New York City's Central Park and the naming of the WW II M4 Sherman tank. Vince Lombardi was right—in America winning isn't everything. It's the only thing.

Leopold II of Belgium (1835-1909)

King Leopold II believed foreign colonies were vital to a nation's greatness and he labored hard to acquire such lands for Belgium. But the Belgian people were not interested in colonies, so Leopold decided to obtain an overseas outpost through his unofficial role of ordinary citizen. The Belgian government loaned him money for the enterprise.

In 1876, Leopold hired the famous explorer Henry Morton Stanley to establish a colony in the Congo region. Nine years later, Leopold was internationally acknowledged as the ruler of the Congo Free State (now the Democratic Republic of the Congo), an area 76 times larger than Belgium. This new nation was Leopold's to rule as his personal domain.

Their Belgian bosses enslaved and methodically abused the people of the Congo Free State as they labored hard for meager wages to build the country's infrastructure and transport rubber and ivory from the interior to the river ports. Workers who could not meet their daily production quotas were often whipped and beaten. Many were mutilated. One missionary was so upset by the terrible conditions he observed in the Congo, he wrote the following to Leopold's chief agent there: "I have just returned from a journey inland to the village of Insongo Mboyo. The abject misery and utter abandon is positively indescribable. I was so moved, Your Excellency, by the people's stories that I took the liberty of promising them that in future you will only kill them for crimes they commit."

In the early 1900s, reports of outrageous maltreatment and pervasive human rights abuses in the Congo led to an international protest movement to expose Leopold's "secret society of murderers." Mark Twain did his part by writing a political satire titled *King Leopold's Soliloquy*, in which the king argues that bringing Christianity to the Congo outweighs a little starvation and the extermination of entire villages. Booker T. Washington, in an article titled "Cruelty in the Congo Country," said, "There was never anything in American slavery that could be compared to the barbarous conditions existing today in the Congo Free State." In 1908, after an estimated two to fifteen million Congolese had perished, the Belgian parliament finally compelled Leopold to give the Congo Free State over to Belgium.

Historians of the era have been quite critical of Leopold. One British historian portrayed him as "an Attila in modern dress" and said "it would have been better for the world if he had never been born." Fellow emperor Franz Joseph of Austria-Hungary called Leopold a "thoroughly bad man." Leopold's subjects expressed their disapproval with him more viscerally. They booed the king during his burial parade.

These days, many Belgians look up to Leopold for the commissioning of a great number of buildings and urban projects all over Belgium. And in the Congo, statues have been erected in his honor. I guess time heals all wounds, except those that are fatal.

JAY GOULD (1836-1892)

Jay Gould was a corrupt and deceitful 19th-century robber baron. He would often dupe his rivals into believing they had beaten him on a transaction and then he would find a legal or contractual ambiguity to overturn the deal. He also pioneered the now commonplace practice of declaring bankruptcy as a calculated maneuver, and he used stock manipulation and insider trading (which were then permissible but not looked upon kindly) to build his wealth and to implement or thwart hostile takeovers.

Gould grew up in relative poverty and received little formal education, but he possessed a quick mind and searched for opportunities to make money. In the 1850s he began speculating in railroad securities.

In 1867, Gould became a director of the Erie Railroad and its president a year after that. These positions helped Gould to profit handsomely from the "Erie Railroad War," in which he and a couple of shady associates, who treated the Erie as nothing but a vehicle for stock manipulation, swindled Cornelius "Commodore" Vanderbilt, who was trying to gain control of the Erie, out of more than seven million dollars. Gould kept out of jail in this affair by sailing across the Hudson River, eluding New York City marshals who had come to arrest him, and setting up Erie corporate headquarters, which had been in New York, in New Jersey.

In 1869, Gould attempted to corner the gold market by buying significant quantities of gold and by paying off President Ulysses S. Grant's brother-in-law to keep Grant from meddling with his scheme. The result was the "Black Friday" panic of 1869, in which many a financial fortune was wiped out. The *Iowa City Daily Citizen,* commenting on the Black Friday Panic, noted, "Failures and suicides followed hard on each other, and nothing but the vigorous efforts of Vanderbilt and Drew, aided by the wise assistance of the government, stemmed the tide that bade fair to bear the soundest into bankruptcy." Gould emerged from the fiscal carnage unscathed. He even made a profit.

From 1868-1888, Gould was involved in many of the largest railway financial operations in the United States. During the Great Southwest Railroad Strike of 1886 he hired strikebreakers. According to labor unionists, he said at the time, "I can hire one half of the working class to kill the other half."

Many Gilded Age capitalists did not trust Gould, and lots of them expressed disdain for his unscrupulous approach to commerce. Not so, Standard Oil President John D. Rockefeller. He said Gould was the most skilled businessman he ever encountered. Evidence of that skill can be adduced from the fact that when Gould died in 1892 he was one of the richest men on the planet. (In a recent inflation-adjusted ranking of America's wealthiest men, Bill Gates scored an anemic 31 on a list led by John D. Rockefeller, Cornelius Vanderbilt and John Jacob Astor. Not far behind, at No. 8, was Jay Gould.)

At his death Gould's fortune was conservatively estimated, for tax purposes, at $72 million (in today's dollars he would be a billionaire). He willed none of that money to charity, which didn't surprise anybody. Gould's favorite charity was himself.

JESSE JAMES (1847-1882)

In the spring of 1864, when he was seventeen, Jesse James joined a murderous group of guerrilla fighters led by "Bloody Bill" Anderson. They terrorized pro-unionists in the Missouri countryside, committing multiple atrocities that included the notorious Centralia massacre, in which 22 unarmed Union army soldiers and 150 other federals were slaughtered. These clashes deeply influenced young Jesse's view of the world.

After the war, Jesse chose to keep on fighting, targeting a bank in Gallatin, Missouri, that was run by the man who had killed Bill Anderson. On December 7, 1869, Jesse and his brother Frank rode into Gallatin, shot an unarmed cashier, and made off with some loot. Eluding a posse sent to capture them, the James boys declared that "they would never be taken alive." The newspapers played up their bravado and Jesse soon began planning his robberies to attract as much notice as possible, including leaving press releases behind at the scenes of his crimes.

With help from John Edwards, an ex-Confederate soldier and newspaper editor, Jesse worked hard at building a myth that portrayed him as a kind of Robin Hood who was helping downtrodden Missourians suffering under the yoke of Reconstruction government. In letters that Edwards published, Jesse asserted: "We are not thieves, we are bold robbers. I am proud of the name, for Alexander the Great was a bold robber, and Julius Caesar, and Napoleon Bonaparte."

During the early 1870s, Jesse and his gang successfully held up a number of banks, stagecoaches and trains. But in September 1876, he made a bad misjudgment while attempting a bank robbery in Northfield, Minnesota. The robbery was a fiasco, leaving two robbers and two innocent victims dead. Jesse and Frank got away but had to hightail it to Tennessee where they took on assumed names.

Jesse tried to settle down but he was restless for the spotlight. In 1879, he formed a new gang. But years had gone by and the public was no longer interested in Robin Hood tales featuring an ex-Confederate outlaw.

On April 3, 1882, a member of Jesse's gang shot him in the back of the head, which, if you're going to be killed, is better than being shot in the front of the head. The murder was a national sensation and as time went on the myth of Jesse James replaced the actual details of his brutal life. Today, swayed by positive depictions in the popular media (e.g., the 2007 movie *The Assassination of Jesse James by the Coward Robert Ford*), many Americans consider Jesse James a romantic figure and folk hero. As a skilled practitioner in the fine art of impression management, I'm sure Jesse would have appreciated this triumph of perception over reality.

Each year in September, a Jesse James Festival is held in Kearney, Missouri, Jesse's boyhood home and final resting place. A carnival, parade, rodeo, historic re-enactments, teen dance, craft exhibits, and barbecue cook-off provide activities for all ages. Kearney is also home to an organization known as "Friends of the James Farm." For Jesse James, the wrong side of the law was indubitably the right place to be.

KAISER WILHELM II (1859-1941)

Prince Wilhelm II, ruler of the German Empire and Prussia from 1888-1918, was born with a deformed left arm. To strengthen that limb he engaged in rigorous exercise as a child, which allowed him to inflict a great deal of pain on others when he had to shake hands. But that pain was nothing compared to the hurt he inflicted on the world through German aggression in World War I.

Although Wilhelm led his nation into the Great War, his impatience and tendency to act on sentiment made him ill equipped to guide German policy during the conflict. As the war progressed his lack of emotional control and military know-how led Wilhelm to rely increasingly on his generals. But he remained a useful figurehead as he toured the front lines, visited munitions plants, awarded medals, and gave rousing speeches.

In 1918, with the German public starving and demoralized and with the German army in great disarray, cries went out for Wilhelm to sue for peace. He refused to even consider the idea. However, he was forced to abdicate when General Wilhelm Groener informed him that the officers and men of the German army would not fight for his throne on the home front. He then quickly took up residence in a small Dutch castle, which enabled him to escape war crimes prosecution, as Queen Wilhelmina, who had family links to Wilhelm, would not extradite him.

In 1919, Wilhelm denounced his abdication as "egged on and misled by the tribe of Juda...Let no German ever forget this, nor rest until these parasites have been destroyed and exterminated from German soil!" He argued for a "regular international all-worlds pogrom 'à la Russe'" as "the best cure" and asserted that Jews are a "nuisance that humanity must get rid of some way or other. I believe the best would be gas!"

In the 1930s, hoping that the rise of the Nazis would stimulate some interest in reviving the monarchy, Wilhelm had his wife petition the Nazi government on his behalf. But the scorn Hitler felt for the man whom he believed had contributed to the fatherland's greatest defeat, plus Hitler's own desire to run the country, prevented Wilhelm's reinstallation. The Fuehrer did, however, at a later date, adopt the Kaiser's notion to gas the Jews.

Wilhelm died of a pulmonary embolism on June 4, 1941, and was buried in a mausoleum in Doorn, Netherlands. The tomb has since become something of a shrine for adherents of the extreme German right and a small but enthusiastic number of German monarchists, who gather there every year on the anniversary of Wilhelm's death to pay homage to the last German emperor. Apparently, for some in Germany, hope for autocracy springs eternal.

BELLE GUNNESS (1859-UNKNOWN)

Belle Gunness was one of America's most wanton serial killers. She murdered most of her beaus, boyfriends, and two of her daughters. And she probably killed her two husbands and the rest of her children as well. Belle's motives involved collecting life insurance benefits. (Her sister said, "Belle was crazy for money. It was her great weakness.") Reports estimate that she murdered more than twenty people over several decades.

Mads Sorenson, a man Belle married in 1884, was most likely her first victim. He died on July 30, 1900, the only day when two life insurance policies on him overlapped. Soon thereafter, two of Belle's young daughters died. Both children were insured.

Belle married Peter Gunness on April 1, 1902. One week later, Peter's infant daughters passed away of unknown causes while alone in the house with Belle. Nine months after that, Peter had a "tragic accident" when, according to Belle, part of a sausage-grinding machine came down on his head in a shed in which he was working and killed him instantly. Belle received $3000 as a result of Peter's death.

In 1906, Belle got engaged to Ray Lamphere, a handyman who performed chores for her. Around the same time, she placed an advertisement in the personals columns of several midwestern newspapers, requesting male companionship. Fifty-year-old John Moo responded to the ad by going to Belle's farm with more than $1,000 to pay off her mortgage. He disappeared within a week of his arrival.

The suitors kept popping in to the Gunness farm but very few popped out. All the while, Belle was having great big trunks sent to her home. In December 1907, Belle replied to a note from Andrew Helgelien by asking him to stop by for a visit. Helgelien brought with him $2,900, which he and Belle took to the bank to cash. Helgelien vanished a few days later.

On April 28, 1908, Belle's house went up in flames. When the fire was extinguished four bodies were found in the cellar. One of the bodies was that of a woman who could not immediately be identified as Belle, as she had no head.

When doctors examined the corpse they determined it was that of a five-foot-three inch 150-pound woman. Testimony from friends and neighbors indicated that Belle was taller than 5'8" and weighed between 180 and 200 pounds. The remains of more than forty men and children buried in shallow graves were also found on Belle's property.

For thirty years after the fire, people reported Belle Gunness sightings in towns and cities throughout the United States. But Belle was never found. Today she's become part of American folklore, a "lady Bluebeard."

LIZZIE BORDEN (1860-1927)

On the morning of August 4, 1892, Lizzie Borden's father, Andrew Jackson Borden, and her stepmother, Abby Borden, were murdered in their family residence in Fall River, Massachusetts. The only other people in the house at the time were Lizzie and the family maid. Lizzie's older sister Emma was away from home.

Both daughters had been upset about their father switching their inheritance over to Abby. Five years before the murders, when Andrew put a rental house in Abby's name, Lizzie and Emma became so enraged that Andrew bought each daughter a house of equal value to Abby's. Emma and Lizzie had quit eating with their parents and referred to Abby as "Mrs. Borden."

In 1891, cash and jewelry were stolen from the master bedroom in the Borden home. It was an open secret that Lizzie was suspected as having been the thief. Several local merchants had also accused Lizzie of shoplifting.

Shortly before the killings a heated family argument occurred, which resulted in both Emma and Lizzie leaving the house on extended "breaks." Lizzie, however, decided to return early, choosing to stay in a rooming house for four days, rather than in her own room in the family residence. On the night before the murders, Lizzie visited a neighbor, Alice Russell, and told her that she feared some unidentified enemy of her father's might soon try to kill him.

The police were never able to find any blood-soaked clothing. (A few days after the murder, Lizzie ripped apart and burned a blue cotton dress in the kitchen stove, saying she had brushed against fresh baseboard paint that had smeared it.) And no murder weapon was found. These details led the jury in the case to have "reasonable doubt" over Lizzie's guilt, and they voted for acquittal after just an hour's deliberation.

Some say Lizzie's exoneration was aided by the fact that her original inquest testimony was excluded from the trial. Also barred was evidence that she tried to buy prussic acid (a powerful poison) from a local drugstore a day before the murders—the druggist refused the sale. Others say the all-male jury was in denial that a Sunday school teacher from a wealthy and respected family could possibly have committed such a horrifying act. That there was another ax murder in the area, which took place directly before the trial, was a piece of good luck for Lizzie.

The trial received lots of national publicity. It has been compared to the OJ Simpson trial as a singular event in legal media coverage. And like the Simpson trial—which produced that unforgettable line "If it doesn't fit, you must acquit"—the Borden trial was also memorialized through catchy language. To wit:

> Lizzie Borden took an axe
> And gave her mother forty whacks.
> And when she saw what she had done
> She gave her father forty-one.

After her hearing Lizzie bought a mansion in Fall River where she lived quite nicely on her father's money. She employed a housekeeper, maid and chauffeur and made regular trips to New York and Boston to take in the theater and concerts. Who says crime doesn't pay?

JACK THE RIPPER (?-?)

Beginning in early 1888, several brutal murders took place in London's East End. The homicides, which involved cutting and mutilating the victims and leaving their bodies in public places, were widely reported in the newspapers. At the same time of the killings, the media and Scotland Yard were receiving letters from an unknown person or persons claiming responsibility for the crimes.

The police inquiry focused on eleven murders that took place in the Whitechapel district between 1888-1891. Five of those murders, "the canonical five," are generally accepted within the Ripperology community, a group composed of professionals and amateurs who have studied the Whitechapel slayings, as almost definitely having been done by the same person. Various writers and historians have also linked at least seven other murders to Jack the Ripper.

Frustrated with police efforts to solve the killings, a group of citizens called the Whitechapel Vigilance Committee began to patrol the streets of London looking for suspicious individuals. They appealed to the government to establish a reward for information about the murderer and engaged private detectives to question witnesses. But their efforts at finding the fiend proved futile.

Newspapers around the world trumpeted the shocking details surrounding the notorious East End butchery. To hype their stories and sell more copies, journalists coined the name "Jack the Ripper." Today, such sensational labeling (e.g., the Boston Strangler, the Beltway Sniper, the Axeman of New Orleans) has become standard media operating procedure.

The murders did have one positive effect in that they brought community attention to the poor of London's East End, which helped English social reformers publicize the plight of the needy. George Bernard Shaw, sarcastically commenting on the sudden concern of the press for the less fortunate, wrote, "Whilst we Social Democrats were wasting our time on education, agitation and organization, some independent genius has taken the matter in hand, and by simply murdering and disemboweling four women, converted the proprietary press to an inept sort of communism."

Jack the Ripper was never captured and has gone on to become the most famous serial killer in history. Over 200 non-fiction books have been published dealing exclusively with his slayings, making them one of the most written-about true crime subjects ever. For those interested in learning more about the Whitechapel murders, *The Complete History of Jack the Ripper* by Philip Sugden offers an excellent overview of the subject.

In 2006, the *BBC History Magazine* and its readers selected Jack the Ripper as the worst Briton in the past thousand years. (Thomas Becket, whose 12th-century conflict with Henry II over the Church divided England, came in a distant second.) That worst Briton was lucky he wasn't caught a hundred years ago. They hung murderers in the UK back then.

JOSEF STALIN (1878-1953)

Josef Stalin, a merciless sociopath responsible for killing 20 to 25 million people, was in his salad days a virtuoso at bank robbery, the protection rackets, arson and piracy. He was a ladies' man as well, fathering a number of illegitimate children. And he wrote poetry and trained as a priest, both by the time he was in his mid-twenties. But his real talent lay in slaughtering people, an aptitude he had the good fortune to indulge in for most of his adult life.

Stalin was a nimble politician and when Lenin died, he was able to outmaneuver his rivals and assume Lenin's mantle as leader of the USSR in 1924. In the 1930s, he solidified his hold on the country with a Great Purge of the Communist Party, a massive eradication campaign that involved expulsions, imprisonments, and executions (e.g., in 1940, Stalin arranged to have Leon Trotsky, a leading opponent of his, murdered in Mexico with an ice pick).

No part of society was left untouched during Stalin's purges. Article 58 of the legal code, listing prohibited "anti-Soviet activities," was applied in the broadest manner and thousands of Russians were murdered as "enemies of the people." Historians have calculated that in the course of Stalin's annihilation campaigns, nearly 700,000 individuals were put to death. (Stalin instinctively understood that most people are not able to fathom such high numbers. He once said, "A single death is a tragedy, six million deaths is a statistic.")

Hundreds of thousands of Russians were also killed shortly before, during, and immediately after World War II, when Stalin conducted a series of expulsions on a huge scale, significantly altering the ethnic map of the

USSR. The banishments took place in abysmal conditions, often by cattle truck. It is estimated that between 1941 and 1949 nearly 3.3 million people were deported to the Central Asian republics and Siberia—a region with the coldest recorded temperature on earth. (Because of Russia's northerly location its citizens never get exiled to nice warm places.)

Mega-megalomaniac that he was, Stalin formed a personality cult around himself that became the focus of great adoration. Numerous Soviet villages and cities were renamed after him, and he accepted larger-than-life titles like "Brilliant Genius of Humanity," "Gardener of Human Happiness," and "Father of Nations." At the same time, he insisted that he be remembered for "the extraordinary modesty characteristic of truly great people." (Such modesty didn't stop Stalin from having his name written into the Soviet national anthem or from rewriting history by providing himself with a more significant role in the revolution.)

In recent years, reverence for "Uncle Joe" has reemerged. Millions of Russians, fed up with the economic and social instability that has come about after the fragmentation of the Soviet Union, want Stalin back. In one poll a substantial minority of Russians said they would vote for Stalin if he were still alive, and Russian history textbooks in 2007 described Stalin as "the most successful Russian ruler of the 20th century." Some see this as a renewal of Stalin's cult. Makes sense to me. It's not easy to keep a bad man down.

Rafael Trujillo (1891-1961)

Rafael Trujillo led the Dominican Republic from 1930 to 1961. Popularly known as "El Jefe" (The Chief), Trujillo was privately called "Chapitas" (bottlecaps) due to the heaps of medals that he wore on his uniform. His tyrannical rule, known as "The Trujillo Era," was one of the bloodiest of the 20th century.

In his youth, Trujillo was a cattle rustler, forger and embezzler. But he was also a soldier, and in 1918 his military career took off when he was accepted into the American-administered Dominican National Guard. He rose rapidly through their ranks, eventually becoming head of the Dominican Army. In 1930, he achieved an even higher position, becoming president of the Dominican Republic in a disputed election in which he received 95 percent of the vote.

Upon taking office, Trujillo decreed that his political party, the Dominican Party, would be the only political group in the country. Those who did not contribute to or join the Dominican Party did so at their own peril, which included being killed. In 1934, when he was up for re-election, Trujillo decided to abolish formal voting altogether. He opted instead for "civic reviews," which basically consisted of large crowds screaming their support for him.

In 1936, the Dominican Congress voted overwhelmingly to rename Santo Domingo, the nation's capital, Ciudad Trujillo. That same year, the province of San Cristóbal was designated as "Trujillo" and the country's highest peak, Pico Duarte, was relabeled Trujillo. Statues, government buildings, bridges—

anything inanimate and in the public domain—could be branded with the Dominican dictator's surname.

In 1937, Trujillo accused the Haitian government of harboring his former Dominican opponents and he ordered an attack on the border. Thousands of Haitians were slaughtered as they attempted to escape. The number of the dead is unknown but it is estimated at between 8,000 and 15,000.

Trujillo used fear and torture to maintain his dictatorship, and he engaged in violent methods abroad. For example, to counter outspoken opposition from Venezuelan president Rómulo Betancourt, Trujillo ordered Dominican foreign agents to plant a bomb near Betancourt's car. The execution attempt, which was carried out on June 24, 1960, injured but did not kill the Venezuelan president. Sadly, the same cannot be said for the 1954 Oldsmobile in which the explosive was placed.

Trujillo was assassinated on May 30, 1961, very likely with CIA assistance. Though being snuffed out may not be the best way to end one's career, the time Trujillo had in power was certainly a lengthy one—31 years. And while his family was voted off the island shortly after his demise, there are some Dominicans around today who defend Trujillo, pining for the tranquility and order that he brought to the nation even if that meant some pain and suffering for themselves and their fellow citizens. A long tenure in office and ardent admirers: El Jefe had them both.

MAO TSE TUNG (1893-1976)

Mao Tse Tung, the leader of the People's Republic of China from its establishment in 1949 until his death in 1976, came to power with Russian government assistance that helped him to defeat the Nationalist Chinese army, which had been weakened from fighting the Japanese in World War II. Had the Russians not given him arms and had Chiang Kai-shek, the Nationalist Chinese leader, not been so inept in chasing him down, Mao might be remembered today simply as a reasonably good poet and calligrapher.

Mao's first political campaigns after founding the People's Republic were land reform and the suppression of counter-revolutionaries through mass executions and other forms of murder. Analyzing the human cost of these actions, the US State Department estimated that there might have been a million killed in Mao's land reform crusade and 800,000 killed in the counter-revolutionary operation. Even in a nation as densely populated as China, that's a whole lot of cadavers.

In 1958, Mao ordered the implementation of a number of untested and unscientific new agricultural techniques by specially formed communes, a program that was labeled the *Great Leap Forward*. The result was the largest famine in human history, with tens of millions of Chinese peasants dying of starvation between 1959 and 1962. Many children, who became emaciated and sick due to having little or nothing to eat during the years of the *Great Leap Forward*, died shortly after the program came to an end in 1962.

In 1966, Mao launched the *Cultural Revolution,* a plan intended to reduce the "menace" of liberal "bourgeois" elements in society. With *Red Guards* in the revolutionary forefront, millions of individuals were prosecuted and punished, schools were shuttered, and young intellectuals living in cities were sent to the countryside to do forced manual labor (which from a glass-is-half-full perspective means they didn't have to join a health club for exercise).

The Revolution led to the destruction of much of China's cultural heritage and the imprisonment of large numbers of Chinese citizens. Millions of lives were ruined and hundreds of thousands, perhaps millions, perished in the savagery of the period. When Mao learned that some people had been driven to suicide he was not very empathetic: "People who try to commit suicide — don't attempt to save them!... China is such a populous nation, it is not as if we cannot do without a few people."

Many historians and academics have been critical of Mao, particularly noting his numerous campaigns to suppress political enemies and trample on human liberties. Some have compared him to Hitler and Stalin. But other scholars have praised Mao for helping China to become a world power and for improving women's rights by abolishing prostitution. And Mao is still officially venerated in his homeland—in the mid-1990s his picture was placed on new Chinese renminbi currency—which leads me to conclude that Abraham Lincoln was correct when he said you can fool some of the people all of the time.

Mohammad Amin al-Husayni

(1895-1974)

Mohammad Amin al-Husayni hated Jews and in April 1920 he showed his dislike of them by inciting large crowds of his fellow Arabs in Jerusalem to kill the Hebrews. For his role in the riots, al-Husayni was sentenced to ten years' imprisonment in absentia (he had fled to Transjordan). However, in 1921, following the death of his brother, a former Jerusalem mufti, al-Husayni was pardoned by the British High Commissioner and appointed Grand Mufti of Jerusalem.

In 1929, Jewish communities in Palestine were subjected to brutal Arab assaults, which at Hebron and Safed ended in massacres. In reviewing the uprisings, the League of Nations Permanent Mandates Commission said that al-Husayni's false accusations against the Jews significantly fueled the insurrection. A British government investigator further declared that al-Husayni had not exercised his authority as a religious leader in restraining the aggression.

On April 19, 1936, a new wave of Arab violence against the Jews broke out in Palestine. To keep the bloodshed going, al-Husayni took money that he was supposed to have spent on education and orphanages and spent it instead on recruiting Arab guerrilla fighters. The conflict lasted three years and only stopped when British troops were brought in to quell the aggression.

When Hitler came to power, al-Husayni sent a telegram to the German Consul-General in Palestine saying it would be his great pleasure to spread

Nazi ideology in the Middle East. The proposal was initially dismissed, out of German concern for upsetting Anglo-German relations. But in 1938 it was accepted, and Germany and Italy sent al-Husayni financial and military support.

In November 1940, Winston Churchill authorized the Irgun, a militant Zionist group, to murder the mufti. Six months later several Irgun members, including former leader David Raziel, were released from prison and flown to Iraq to assassinate al-Husayni. However, the plan had to be abandoned when a German plane killed Raziel.

During World War II, al-Husayni worked for the Nazis as a propagandist to stir up Arab public opinion and to recruit of Muslim volunteers for the German armed forces. He was also involved in the organization and recruitment of Bosnian Muslims into several divisions of the Waffen SS. And he made radio broadcasts from Berlin imploring Arabs to "kill the Jews wherever you find them."

After the war, a Yugoslav military court sentenced al-Husayni to three years in prison. In 1948, he escaped and was given asylum in Egypt. There he did what he could to stir up hatred against the Jews.

Al-Husayni died in Beirut, Lebanon on July 4, 1974. He had wanted to be buried in Jerusalem, but the Israeli government refused his request. That may have been because of the way it was worded. I suspect the Israeli government would have gladly granted al-Husayni his petition if they could have buried him *alive*.

CHARLES "LUCKY" LUCIANO (1897-1962)

Charles "Lucky" Luciano was a Sicilian-American mobster and the first "official" boss of the Genovese crime family. *Time* magazine named him one of the top 20 most influential builders and titans of the 20th century. He is considered the father of modern organized crime.

In 1919, when Luciano was twenty-two, the 18th amendment was passed to the US Constitution, making Prohibition the law of the land. The following year, Luciano and a number of mafia big shots went into the bootlegging business in New York City. By 1925, Luciano and his associates had become the largest suppliers of illegal alcohol in the Big Apple.

Not all gangsters were happy with Luciano's good fortune. That displeasure was made evident one day in 1929 when three men shoved Luciano into a limo, where he was beaten and stabbed before being dumped on a New York Harbor beach. Lucky for Luciano he survived the ordeal. And his good fortune was just beginning.

In the 1930s, Luciano was in charge of the most powerful crime family in America. Its underground policy set geographical boundaries, distributed crime profits, and enforced its edicts with the help of Murder, Inc., an organized crime group that carried out hundreds of murders on behalf of the mob. Luciano made the rules and woe unto those who crossed them. One of his edicts was "we only kill each other." When Dutch Schultz tried to rub out a district attorney in violation of that decree, Schultz was executed in the DA's place.

In 1936, Luciano was convicted on a number of charges and sent to prison. That didn't slow him down. He continued to run the Luciano crime family from the penitentiary, relaying his orders through Vito Genovese, his first acting boss.

During World War II, the US government used Luciano's mafia contacts to search for German saboteurs in the ports of New York and to furnish intelligence to American forces as they moved through the Italian peninsula. As payback for his cooperation, Luciano was allowed to run his criminal operations from jail. In 1946, Luciano was paroled on the condition that he go to Sicily. He secretly moved to Cuba instead where he continued to control American mafia operations.

In his later years, Luciano lived it up in Naples, dining at the city's finest eateries and dwelling in deluxe apartments with Igea Lissoni, a dancer and nightclub employee who became the love of his life. He also indulged in a little philanthropy, giving money to indigent Italians while setting up a medical supply store as a front for his illicit dealings.

In 1962, Luciano's luck ran out when he died of a heart attack at Naples International Airport (he had gone there to meet a Hollywood producer). But in death he was allowed to come back to the United States, the country he considered his only true home. In 1972, more than ten years after his passing, Luciano was permitted interment at St. John's Cemetery in New York City, the town that gave him his big start on the road to criminal fame and criminal fortune.

HIROHITO (1901-1989)

Hirohito was the emperor of Japan from 1926 until his death in 1989. Of the three World War II Axis leaders, he was the only one left alive and in office at the end of the war. And he lived 44 years after that.

In 1931, Japan invaded Manchuria, and six years later, the rest of China. Primary sources indicate that Hirohito never objected to these attacks, which were recommended to him by his chiefs of staff and prime minister. He also authorized the use of chemical weapons against the Chinese and approved the assault on the United States naval base at Pearl Harbor that led to Japan and the US being drawn into World War II, humanity's deadliest war, causing tens of millions of deaths. (The civilian toll was around 47 million, including 20 million deaths due to war-related famine and disease. The military toll was about 25 million, including the deaths of about four million prisoners of war in captivity.)

Following their capitulation to the Allies in 1945, the Japanese depicted Hirohito as a powerless figurehead who had behaved strictly according to protocol while remaining at a distance from the decision-making processes. But historical research by Professor Herbert P. Bix—see *Hirohito and the Making of Modern Japan*—indicates that Hirohito was deeply engaged in the daily running of Japanese military operations during World War II. Professor Bix points out that the Imperial General Headquarters was put inside the Imperial Palace to assist Hirohito in executing his constitutional role as supreme commander of Japan's armed forces. Through Imperial General

Headquarters, Hirohito was able to participate directly in war planning and assess how the war was proceeding.

When Japan surrendered, the Australian government wanted to prosecute Hirohito as a war criminal. But General Douglas MacArthur, the Supreme Commander of the Allied Powers, had a different idea. He believed managing a defeated Japan would be a lot easier if the emperor appeared to be cooperating with the occupying Allied forces. That could not happen if the emperor was charged and convicted of war crimes. President Truman backed MacArthur's view, so due to political reasons, Japan's chief war criminal avoided prosecution and probable execution.

For the rest of his life Hirohito was an active public figure, carrying out numerous duties commonly connected with heads of state. He and his family performed ribbon cuttings and made special appearances at civic events and ceremonies. The emperor especially liked going to sumo wrestling matches, where, sitting in the imperial box, he carefully noted the winners and losers.

Hirohito traveled abroad from time to time to meet with foreign leaders such as American presidents and the British queen. In 1975, Hirohito and his wife were honored guests at Colonial Williamsburg in Virginia, a first-time visit there by Japanese royalty. I very much doubt Hitler and Mussolini would have been extended a similar invitation to visit a top tourist attraction in the Old Dominion state had they survived the war.

ALBERT SPEER (1905-1981)

At the war-crimes trials of Nazi leaders in Nuremberg, Albert Speer—the Fuehrer's Armaments Minister and fave architect—was sentenced to 20 years in Berlin's Spandau prison for colluding in Hitler's butchery. Unlike his codefendants, most of whom were hanged, Speer voluntarily accepted blame for crimes committed by an immoral government in which he played a key part. But he maintained it was not until the trial that he learned about the mass murders that went on in German concentration camps. Speer wrote his daughter in 1952, "Of the dreadful things, I knew nothing." Can you say liar, liar, pants on fire!

Speer joined the National Socialist Party in 1931. Soon thereafter he became a highly respected member of Hitler's inner circle—the Fuehrer, who had once had architectural ambitions himself, particularly prized those he considered fellow artists. Named the Fatherland's war-production czar in 1942, Speer ran the munitions factories where hundreds of thousands of slave laborers died of overwork and malnutrition. Reports show that by September 1944, some 7.5 million foreigners were working as slave laborers. (These included two million prisoners of war, a group prohibited from such work by The Hague and Geneva Conventions.) Speer was personally responsible for rounding up and "resettling" at least 75,000 Jews from Berlin, most of whom were later murdered.

As the fighting went on, Speer, ever the consummate professional, became more efficient at his job. The production of German war materiel actually increased under his direction while the war was winding down. These additional military supplies prolonged the agony of those on the battlefields.

When he was released from prison in 1966, Speer published two self-serving memoirs, *Inside the Third Reich* and *The Secret Diaries*, which became hugely successful in Germany and helped Speer to become a rich man. Many in Deutschland believed his story about not knowing what was going on at Auschwitz, Dachau, Treblinka, and the other German death camps. But to many skeptics, Speer's statements at Nuremberg and in his best-selling memoirs suggested that Hitler's chum was in deep denial.

Speer's oldest supporter during his years behind bars, Rudolf Wolters, a German architect and Nazi sympathizer, became disenchanted with him after his release. Wolters knew what Speer was concealing. Speer told Wolters that his constant cries of "mea culpa" and his endless expressions of sorrow were only a charade. Wolters wrote, "He himself called them his 'tricks' to my face."

Speer lived to be an old man who enjoyed his freedom into the 1980s. He may never have built "Germania," Hitler's projected renewal of Berlin, which was to have been constructed after Germany's planned victory in World War II, but in the end he won. He survived! To this day Speer remains the ultimate escape artist who strolled out of Nuremberg alive, and later exited prison a free man.

FRANÇOIS DUVALIER (1907-1971)

François Duvalier, aka Papa Doc, was the son of a justice of the peace and a mentally unstable woman who lived in an asylum for much of her life. Raised mostly by an aunt, he earned an MD degree from the University of Haiti in 1934. Duvalier subsequently worked as a doctor and public health officer before becoming president of Haiti, a position he held from 1957 until his death in 1971.

Duvalier had the good luck to be schooled in a country where most people could not read or write. He was also fortunate to have involved himself in Haiti's black pride movement and to have immersed himself in the study of voodoo, Haiti's native faith. His education and religious knowledge paid huge political dividends when he went into politics.

Duvalier became president in a rigged election and once sworn in, he revived the traditions of voodoo. He deliberately modeled his persona on that of Baron Samedi, a voodoo spirit of the dead, and used that role to impress the country's uneducated peasantry. They were duly awed.

To maintain his regime, Duvalier employed private militias nicknamed the Tonton Macoute. Soldiers in these forces were famous for wearing military clothing comparable to Italian Fascist and Nazi attire. They were also famous for wearing dark spectacles, wielding machetes, and leaving their victims hanging in public places as a warning to others.

In 1961, the US cut off most of its economic aid to Haiti because of extensive Haitian government corruption. Duvalier responded by rewriting the constitution and then staging a one-candidate "fixed" election two years before his term was scheduled to end. The official results were 1.32 million votes for Duvalier, none against.

In April 1963, Clement Barbot, the head of the Tonton Macoute, initiated a plot to remove Duvalier from office. The plan failed and Duvalier ordered a massive hunt for Barbot. During the search, Duvalier received information that Barbot had changed himself into a black dog. He responded by decreeing that all black dogs in Haiti be put to death. In another case, Duvalier demanded that the head of a slain rebel be brought to him so he could connect with the dead man's spirit. His bizarre behavior in these episodes won him additional popularity with the proletariat.

In 1964, Duvalier declared himself "President for Life." Shortly thereafter, many of Haiti's educated professionals left their nation for places overseas. Duvalier didn't mind them going, as they were not part of his political base.

As Duvalier's reign progressed, malnutrition and famine became endemic. With most of Haiti's aid money being spent improperly and the Tonton Macoute tossing peasants off their lands, the country was a real mess. But Duvalier continued to maintain substantial support among Haiti's majority black rural population, who saw him as a backer of their claims against the historically dominant mulatto elite.

When Papa Doc died his 19-year-old son, Baby Doc, followed him as Haiti's leader. No surprises here. His rule was as terrible as his father's.

ENVER HOXHA (1908-1985)

Enver Hoxha got involved in politics through a tobacco shop that he ran in Tirana. The store became a secret meeting site for a group of Albanian communists, who helped Hoxha to become the leader of the Albanian Communist Party during World War II. After the war, Hoxha became the leader of Albania as well its foreign minister, defense minister, and army commander in chief.

A huge fan of Stalin, Hoxha imitated his hero by crushing those who opposed him. He replicated the repressive methods of the Russian secret police, launching purges in which his enemies were fired from their jobs, locked up in forced-labor camps, and often put to death. When Hoxha left office (he stayed in power for forty years) one out of three Albanian citizens had either served time in prison camps or been interrogated by the Albanian secret police.

Under Hoxha's rule, Albania became the most closed and isolated nation in Europe. Travel to and from Albania was severely restricted and news from abroad was filtered through government censors. Such curbing of outside influences helped Hoxha to set up a personality cult that celebrated his virtues. He was portrayed as the savior of Albania, given nicknames like "Great Teacher" and "Sole Force," honored through a museum that was dedicated to his life, and commemorated in statues that were erected throughout the country.

In 1967, Hoxha declared Albania the first and only officially atheist state in history and he seized religious buildings. Many churches, mosques and monasteries were promptly gutted, while others were converted into storehouses, stables, machine shops and movie theaters. Hoxha also instructed parents not to give religious names to their children and he prohibited the possession of Korans, Bibles, icons, and religious objects. He did not, however, prohibit people from worshipping him.

In 1976, Hoxha stopped doing business with Communist China, Albania's last remaining trade partner, and Albania became a self-sufficient economy. This action helped Albania to maintain its position as the land with the lowest standard of living in Europe. Bizarrely, the Albanian public had been so cut off from the outside world that they thought their nation had the highest living standard on the continent.

In 1981, to ensure the succession of a younger generation of leaders, Hoxha ordered the execution of several leading party and government officials. Shortly thereafter he went into semiretirement and in 1985 he passed away. Grieved by the death of the only leader most of them had ever known, the Albanian public mourned their loss.

Hoxha was replaced in power by his chosen successor, Ramiz Alia, a kindred spirit on foreign and domestic issues. Hoxha had done what he could to wreck his country. Now it was up to the next guy.

NE WIN (1910-2002)

Ne Win, a child of mixed Chinese-Burmese descent, became involved in the struggle for Burmese independence during the 1930s. This led him to pursue a military career and he eventually became the head of the Burmese army. In 1962, he became the leader of Burma, a position he held till 1988.

Ne Win developed the "Burmese Way to Socialism," a political set of guidelines based on dislike of outsiders, moral rectitude, and superstition. Foreigners were banned from the country, businesses were nationalized, and nearly all entertainment was prohibited. Burma—a prosperous nation with large quantities of timber and gemstones, an educated labor force, and plentiful rice exports—started to suffer in steamy seclusion.

The general public had to endure far more than its leader. After he banned horse racing at home, Ne Win was spotted betting at the Ascot races in England. Though he advocated moderation, Ne Win married five times—including an Italian actress and a descendant of the last Burmese royal family. And while he preached mental toughness, Ne Win regularly visited a psychiatrist in Vienna during the 1960s.

A disciple of Marx and Stalin, Ne Win ruthlessly clamped down on his enemies and clashes between students and the military were common, often with deadly costs for the protestors. In 1987, he removed from circulation much of the nation's money supply in order to introduce new notes in denominations of 45 and 90 kyats because they were divisible by nine (his lucky number). This action wiped out the savings of millions. In 1987, the

UN also designated Burma a "Least Developed Nation," officially recognizing the once affluent country as one of the ten poorest nations in the world.

By March 1988, students were taking their complaints to the streets. Five months later Ne Win resigned, a decision that had wide-ranging consequences, as up to 10,000 demonstrators were killed in an uprising against his government, some with barbaric cruelty. The chief opposition leader, Aung San Suu Kyi, was arrested and put under house arrest, where she remained until 1995, before being detained again between 2000-2002.

In retirement, Ne Win stayed away from directly involving himself in politics, but he still exercised some influence with Burma's ruling military junta. There were reports that he drove around Rangoon at night, an eerie figure checking out the city's empty streets and crumbling colonial buildings. In March 2002, he was put under house arrest for suspicion of taking part in an alleged plot to overthrow the junta.

He didn't remain under house arrest for very long. Ne Win died on December 5, 2002, at the age of 92, at his lakeside home in Yangon. "The Puppet Master,'" "The Old Man," the guy known as "No. 1" had finally departed his native soil.

Ne Win's legacy is a terrible one. Once a wealthy country on the rise, Myanmar (Burma's name changed in 1988) is now a remote and impoverished land. For the beleaguered and bankrupt people of Burma, Ne win was a no win.

JOSEF MENGELE (1911-1979)

Josef Mengele was in charge of the Auschwitz gas chambers and their crematoria for 21 months during World War II. A man of cruel efficiency, when it was reported that one block was infected with lice he solved the problem by gassing all 750 women assigned to it, Mengele was also a bit of a megalomaniac. "He had a look that asserted 'I am the power,'" said one survivor.

Mengele liked to dramatize his murderous policies. In one case he drew a line on the wall of the children's block five feet from the floor and then sent those whose heads could not reach the line to the gas chamber. In another instance, when a mother did not want to be separated from her 13-year-old daughter and bit and scratched the face of an SS man who tried to force her to an assigned spot, Mengele shot both the mother and the child with his pistol. He then sent to the gas all the people who were in the mother's transport, who earlier been chosen for work, saying as they left, "Away with this shit." (In addition to being a brutal and vicious thug, the "Angel of Death" always liked to have the last word.)

Mengele, who was both an SS officer and a physician, viewed Auschwitz as an opportunity to do human experimentation in genetics research. He was particularly interested in twins, who were selected and assigned to special barracks. When an experiment was completed, the twins who took part in it were typically murdered and their bodies dissected.

When the Allied forces came to liberate Auschwitz, Mengele disguised himself as a German infantry soldier. He was subsequently arrested and released from custody, as his captors were not aware whom they were holding. In the fall of 1948, Mengele decided to leave Germany for Argentina, a South American country receptive to ex-Nazis.

In Buenos Aires, Mengele first labored as a construction worker but, after coming into contact with some prominent Germans who were living in the Argentine capital, he was able to ditch such drudgery and have a more comfortable lifestyle. In May 1960, he fled to Paraguay just weeks before the Israeli Mossad operation that abducted Adolf Eichmann could find him. He was a secondary objective in that action.

In the latter years of his life, Mengele lived in a bungalow in a suburb of São Paulo, Brazil. In 1977, Mengele told his son, Rolf, who was visiting his father there that he "had never personally harmed anyone in his whole life." The audacity of that statement staggers the imagination.

Mengele shuffled off this mortal coil on February 7, 1979, in Bertioga, Brazil, where he either accidentally drowned or perhaps suffered a stroke while swimming in the ocean. Couldn't have happened to a more reprehensible guy.

KIM IL-SUNG (1912-1994)

At the beginning of World War II, Kim Il-Sung fought with Chinese Communist guerrilla groups against Japanese soldiers who had invaded China and Korea. He saw lots of action and while many of his companions were killed Kim emerged from the fighting alive. This permitted him to become president of North Korea a few years later, a position he held from 1948 until his death in 1994.

Shortly after becoming president, Kim began promoting the notion of a war of reunification with the South. On June 25, 1950, he launched that war by invading South Korea. When the conflict ended, three years later, three million people had been killed, the infrastructure of North Korea had been largely destroyed, and the two Koreas were still separate states.

In the post-war period, Kim established a work-camp system similar to that used in the Soviet Union for the detention of political prisoners. Today it is estimated that between 150,000 and 200,000 political prisoners are being held in six or seven sprawling complexes called "kwan-li-so" (political penal-labor colonies) in North Korea, where they are being fed only enough food to be kept on the verge of starvation.

Kim ran North Korea like a personal fiefdom. He had statues of himself installed throughout the country, bulletin boards were put up across the land displaying his thoughts, and the people of North Korea were obliged to hang his portrait in their homes. Kim's day of birth was made a national holiday.

In 1982, Kim celebrated his 70th birthday in lavish style by unveiling the Juche Tower (a larger version of the Washington Monument, featuring

25,550 blocks of granite, one for each day of the 70 years of Kim's life), the Arch of Triumph (a larger version of the Arc de Triomphe in Paris, featuring 70 bas-reliefs of azaleas), and the 100,000-seat Kim Il-Sung Stadium. In the meantime, North Korea was going broke.

Kim's rotten management of his nation's economy caused between one to three million deaths from lack of food during his 46-year reign—the level of malnutrition got so bad in North Korea that the army had to lower the minimum height for conscripts. To distract the populace from becoming depressed over not having enough to eat, and to offset energy problems that were brought on by economic problems, Kim invested in nuclear power. That investment paid off.

Today North Korea has the atom bomb. The Worker's Paradise also has thousands of loudspeakers that at 7 a.m. each morning, all across the land, broadcast the song "Ten Million Human Bombs for Kim Il-Sung." In death, as in life, Kim Il-Sung remains a megastar.

Kim 's corpse, which is displayed at a mausoleum in the Kumsusan memorial palace in Pyongyang, has become a tourist attraction. Visitors who want to see Kim's body have to walk around it and bow at every side. There is also a statue of Kim, which visitors are required to pay obeisance to, in the palace. Unlike the late comic Rodney Dangerfield, Kim Il-Sung gets too much respect.

AUGUSTO PINOCHET (1915-2006)

Augusto Pinochet was President of Chile from 1974 to 1990. According to the Chilean government's 1993 National Commission for Truth and Reconciliation Report, 2,279 persons were killed for political reasons under his regime. A companion report states that 30,000 individuals were tortured and several thousand were exiled by the Pinochet administration.

Some of the most infamous cases of human rights violations occurred during the initial stage of Pinochet's coup against Marxist president Salvadore Allende. For example, in October 1973, the Caravan of Death, a Chilean death squad, executed at least 75 people during a three-week period. Two years later, in 1975, a number of government officials who worked for Allende were assassinated outside the country by Pinochet's secret police during *Operation Condor*, a cooperative venture involving a number of South American intelligence agencies and a US communication base in Panama. Also in 1975, at least 119 people were kidnapped and later killed by Chilean government forces in *Operation Colombo*.

In 1986, an armed wing of the Communist Party staged an unsuccessful attempt on Pinochet's life. Five bodyguards were killed and eleven were wounded, but Pinochet escaped unharmed. The failed assassination effort unleashed a new round of military terror against the left.

In March 1990, faced with mounting internal and external opposition to his rule, Pinochet stepped down from the presidency, transferring power to a new democratically elected president. But he stayed on as commander-in-chief of the army and was able to arrange having himself sworn in as senator-for-life, a role that Pinochet wrote into Chile's constitution.

Being a senator shielded Pinochet from deposed complaints against him, and legal challenges only started after he was taken into custody in 1998 in the UK, through an arrest warrant issued by a Spanish judge on abuse charges that had been made many times before his capture, but never acted upon.

The British placed Pinochet under house arrest and initiated judicial proceedings, but he was released for health reasons without facing trial in March 2000. He then went immediately to Chile, where he was indicted on a number of human rights violations. He was never convicted of any of them. The Chilean Supreme Court dismissed the indictments on medical grounds.

Pinochet died on December 10, 2006, at the age of 91, a free man. He also died a wealthy man, largely from money that had been laundered through American banks. But he did not die with the full pomp and ceremony that is normally given to former Chilean presidents. Pinochet was denied a state funeral at his death and was instead provided a military one, as former army commander-in-chief. And the government refused to declare a national day of mourning. I hate to be a nitpicker, but it seems to me that these punishments don't exactly fit the crimes.

ELENA CEAUŞESCU (1916-1989)

Elena Ceauşescu was a self-proclaimed scientist, the Vice Prime Minister of Romania, and the wife of Romanian president Nicolae Ceauşescu. A woman who favored the title "Mother of the nation," Elena was anything but maternal. During the 25 years that her husband ruled Romania she was possibly the most despised person in the country.

On her wedding day (December 23, 1947), Elena forged her birth certificate to make her look younger than Nicolae, who was two years her junior. Such dishonesty was perfectly in character, as reports show that Elena was tossed out of an adult education exam for cheating and she outsourced her PhD dissertation. (Accounts from her graduate school instructors indicate that Elena rarely attended lectures or classes, but instead sent government security agents to drop off her homework, which many doubt she actually worked on.)

Elena liked to travel with Nicolae and in June 1971, on a journey with him to the People's Republic of China, she learned that Mao's wife had a position of actual state power. Not to be outdone by her Asian counterpart, Elena had herself "elected" a member of the Romanian Central Commission on Socio-Economic Forecasting in July 1971 and a member of the Romanian Communist Party Central Committee a year later. In 1977 she was selected to serve on the Permanent Bureau of the Political Executive Committee, the highest party body. Subsequently, she was appointed First Deputy Prime Minister.

Elena was largely responsible for the Romanian government's abolition of birth control that created calamitous conditions during the 1970s and 1980s, resulting in thousands of unwanted children who were placed in shoddy state-run orphanages throughout the country. She also headed the state health commission, which denied the existence of AIDS in Romania, leading to one of the largest outbreaks of that disease in the developed world. In the 1980s, she helped devise policies that resulted in the demolition of churches and food rationing.

When the 1989 Romanian Revolution broke out, Elena and her husband tried to flee from Bucharest but were quickly captured. At their trial, Elena refused to answer questions or acknowledge her interrogators' authority, declaring that they did not know whom they were talking to and that they were speaking in an insulting manner. While those comments probably didn't win her much sympathy among the questioners, they didn't have any real effect on the trial's outcome, as the verdict was prearranged.

On December 25, 1989, with Nicolae singing the Communist national anthem and Elena screaming for everyone to go to hell, the Ceauşescus were executed. Elena was almost 74 years old. For a tomato whose education ended at the fourth grade and who worked as a laboratory assistant before getting a job in a textile factory, I'd say Madame Ceauşescu had a pretty good run.

FERDINAND MARCOS (1917-1989)

In 1939, Ferdinand Marcos was arrested and found guilty of murdering a man in the Philippines. He appealed his conviction, and representing himself before the Philippine Supreme Court, had the decision overturned. That "not guilty" verdict was a great break for Marcos and a disastrous one for the Philippine people.

In 1965, Marcos was elected president of the Philippine Islands. His rule began well, but after five years the public became disenchanted and started to demonstrate. In August 1971, he suspended habeas corpus as a prelude to martial law.

In 1973, a new constitution was put into place, allowing Marcos to stay in office indefinitely. He was also given the authority to appoint all government officials and members of the judiciary. Using that power he selected his wife, Imelda (who later gained worldwide notoriety for her extensive shoe collection—it was rumored that she had at one time more than 3,000 pairs of shoes, although she claimed it was only 1,060), to be governor of Manila.

Between 1972 and 1977, more than 60,000 people were arrested in the Philippines. Political prisoners were routinely tortured and "disappearances" and murders of suspected political activists were common. The brutality of the Marcos government and the declining Philippine economy got so bad that many Filipinos turned to the Communists for protection and support.

In 1983, after three years in exile, opposition leader Benigno Aquino returned to the Philippines to help end the Marcos regime. But minutes after his arrival at the Manila airport he was shot in the head and killed. His lone assassin was immediately gunned down.

Marcos claimed the hit man was a Communist. However, a subsequent government commission found that the military had conspired in Aquino's death. This finding was rejected and those accused of the conspiracy were allowed to go free.

In 1985, with the poor growing poorer and the rich growing richer in the Philippines, Benigno Aquino's widow, Corazón, announced she would run for president. In the election that followed, which was marked by widespread fraud and intimidation, Marcos was victorious. But the people rebelled and on February 25, 1986, Marcos and his wife were forced to abandon the presidential palace. They left on a jet for Hawaii.

When Marcos landed in the Aloha State he was said to be carrying suitcases holding jewels, 24-carat gold bricks, and certificates for billions of dollars in gold bullion. His Swiss bank accounts were estimated to contain between 3 billion and 35 billion dollars stolen from the Philippines. He was, to vastly understate the case, a man of mega-mega means.

In 1988, Marcos was indicted by a federal grand jury in New York for multiple offenses, including mail fraud, fraudulent misappropriation of property, and obstruction of justice. He died of a heart attack before he could be tried.

In 2004, the international anticorruption organization Transparency International placed Marcos second on a list of the world's most corrupt political leaders of the past two decades. Indonesian President Suharto was the only bigger crook. While Marcos may not have been a top ten totalitarian killer, he was without a doubt a world-class authoritarian thief.

LEONA HELMSLEY (1920-2007)

Leona Panzirer was a condominium broker in 1968 when she began going out with the then-married multi-millionaire real estate mogul Harry Helmsley. In 1972, Helmsley divorced his wife of 33 years and married Leona. That union probably salvaged her career, as she was involved in several losing lawsuits and had had her real estate license suspended at the time. To keep going, she focused on managing Harry's hotels.

Leona was featured in an ad campaign for Helmsley hotels, which portrayed her as a benevolent queen who wanted her guests to be treated regally. But in real life Leona was a despotic boss whose bad temper was a poor fit for the hospitality industry. An employee's least mistake was often grounds for getting the boot, and Leona frequently screamed insults and obscenities at targeted workers right before they were fired.

On March 31, 1982, Leona's son, Jay, died of a heart attack. Shortly thereafter the "Queen of Mean" sued her son's estate for money and property that she said he had borrowed. She also served an eviction notice on Jay's widow, Mimi, who was living in a Leona-owned property in Florida. Mimi later said that she was bankrupted by the legal costs and that she never understood why Leona hated her so much.

In 1988, the US Attorney's office indicted the Helmsleys and two of their associates on several tax-related charges, as well as extortion. Due to Harry's ill health, Leona had to face the charges alone.

At the trial, a former Helmsley executive testified that he had refused to sign phony invoices illegally billing the company for work done on Helmsley's

Connecticut mansion. Another witness, a housekeeper at the Helmsley home, told of this exchange with Leona: "I said, 'You must pay a lot of taxes.' She said, 'We don't pay taxes. Only the little people pay taxes.'"

Leona was acquitted of extortion—a charge that could have sent her to prison for the rest of her life—but she was convicted on a number of other counts and sentenced to 16 years in prison. That sentence was eventually reduced and Leona wound up serving just 18 months in jail.

In 2002, Charles Bell, a former employee who alleged that he was discharged solely for being homosexual, sued Leona. The jury in the case found in his favor and ordered her to pay Bell $11.2 million in damages. A judge later cut this amount to a mere $554,000.

Leona died in 2007, with an estate estimated at more than four billion dollars. She left 12 million of those dollars, the single largest bequest in her will, to her dog, a seven-year old Maltese bitch named Trouble, and no money to two grandchildren "for reasons which are known to them." In 2008, a New York City surrogate judge reduced Trouble's trust fund to $2 million and directed the remaining $10 million to go to a charitable foundation. Trouble, who is currently living in Sarasota, Florida, with the general manager of the Helmsley Sandcastle Hotel and suffering from several ongoing medical problems, has not appealed the ruling.

SUHARTO (1921-2008)

On the morning of October 1, 1965, six Indonesian generals were kidnapped and murdered by pro-Communist (PKI) forces in Jakarta. In response, President Sukarno appointed Suharto (like many Javanese, Suharto had only one name) commander of the army, with orders to "clean up" the PKI.

Suharto began his cleansing by cracking down hard on PKI members and their supporters. His forces murdered hundreds of thousands of them. He also purged the parliament and military of pro-Sukarno loyalists. This latter action politically and militarily isolated Sukarno.

On March 11, 1966, Sukarno, who was in poor health, transferred supreme authority to Suharto to do whatever was needed to restore calm to the country. This edict virtually assured Suharto the presidency, as he was now able to exercise total power over the Indonesian parliament. A year later that legislative body installed Suharto as acting president. He was elected president by the parliament a year after that.

Once in office, Suharto quickly put into place new economic policies that redirected private investment and government funds to himself and his cronies. He also established two powerful intelligence agencies to deal with threats to his regime, and he greatly expanded the powers of the Indonesian government.

In 1970, political and economic corruption led to student demonstrations and the formation of a government commission to examine charges of wrongdoing. Suharto responded by outlawing student protests and prosecuting a tiny number of the cases that were recommended by the commission. This pattern of criminalizing behavior that he didn't like and offering token justice became a trademark of Suharto's administration.

In the 1980s, corruption continued as a major issue. Ties to Suharto were considered essential for doing business in Indonesia, with those in favor being given lucrative government contracts regardless of performance. Suharto's six children also became involved in dubious business practices, and his wife was given the moniker "Madame Ten Percent," a nod to the fee that she was demanding from business transactions.

In 1998, with Indonesia facing massive fiscal problems and its government embroiled in accusations of deception and fraud, Suharto stood for reelection. As in previous years, he ran unopposed. But this time rioting and protesting by the Indonesian people forced him to step down from the presidency. He left that post with an overabundance of assets. In May 1999, *Time Asia* calculated Suharto's family fortune at $15 billion in cash, stock, corporate securities, real estate, jewelry and fine art. Transparency International has estimated that Suharto embezzled more money than any other world leader in history—a probable $15–35 billion during his 32-year rule.

In 2000, Indonesian authorities placed Suharto under house arrest and began to look into corruption during his regime. But he never stood trial on corruption charges because his lawyers successfully argued that his various medical conditions prevented him from doing so. The state was forced instead to engage in legal actions against Suharto's family members and former minions. To date those measures have been highly unsuccessful. Chalk it up as more evidence of good things happening to bad people.

JESSE HELMS (1921-2008)

Jesse Alexander Helms, Jr. was a five-term Republican US Senator from North Carolina, a chairman of the Senate Foreign Relations Committee, and a person *Washington Post* columnist David Broder has labeled a "white racist."

As an aide to the 1950 Senate campaign of North Carolina Republican candidate Willis Smith, Helms helped create attack ads against Smith's opponent, including one which read: "White people, wake up before it is too late. Do you want Negroes working beside you, your wife and your daughters, in your mills and factories? Frank Graham favors mingling of the races." Another ad featured photographs that Helms had altered to point up the allegation that Graham's wife had danced with a black man.

In his 1984 Senate race, when Helms faced a tough Democratic opponent, he initiated a Senate filibuster against the bill making Martin Luther King Junior's birthday a national holiday. Strom Thurmond, who ran for president in 1948 on the segregationist Dixiecrat ticket, and the majority of the Senate took an opposite stance but with this action Helms was able to halve his election deficit and retain his seat.

In 1990, in the midst of a tight race against an African-American, Helms aired a final-week TV ad that showed a pair of white hands scrunching up a rejection letter, while an announcer said, "You needed that job and you were the best qualified. But they had to give it to a minority because of a racial quota." Once again Helms emerged victorious.

In 1993, Helms sang "Dixie" in an elevator to Carol Moseley-Braun, the first African-American woman elected to the Senate, saying, "I'm going to make her cry. I'm going to sing Dixie until she cries."

In calumnies and commentaries from the Senate chambers, Helms promoted racial hatred and called names: The University of North Carolina was "the University of Negroes and Communists." Of civil rights protests Helms wrote, "The Negro cannot count forever on the kind of restraint that's thus far left him free to clog the streets, disrupt traffic, and interfere with other men's rights." In 1995, when a caller to the *Larry King Live* show lauded guest Jesse Helms for "everything you've done to help keep down the niggers," Helms responded by saying, "Well, thank you, I think."

The press never seriously went after Helms for his racial prejudice because they wanted access to the chairman of one of the Senate's most powerful committees. And now that he's dead there's no reason to suspect that the members of the fourth estate are going to go after him at this point. In his memoir, *Here's Where I Stand,* Helms maintained he was not a racist and claimed, "I have always counted many blacks among my friends." As they say in football country, the best defense is a good offense.

IDI AMIN (CA. 1920S-2003)

In 1946, Idi Amin joined the King's African Rifles (KAR) of the British Colonial Army as an assistant cook. Twenty years later he had risen to become the commander of the Ugandan army. It was as chief of the military that he overthrew Ugandan president Milton Obote in 1971, before Obote could arrest him for misappropriating government funds. Assuming Obote's place as president, Amin later gave himself a more impressive title: *His Excellency President for Life, Field Marshal Al Hadji Doctor Idi Amin, VC, DSO, MC, Lord of All the Beasts of the Earth and Fishes of the Sea, and Conqueror of the British Empire in Africa in General and Uganda in Particular.*

Amin's time in power was marked by political repression, ethnic persecution, human rights abuses, and the expulsion of approximately 60,000 Asians from Uganda. The number of individuals murdered under Amin's rule is unknown, but estimates range from 80,000 to 500,000. Even at the lower figure, that's a heck of a lot of dead Ugandans.

In June 1976, Amin allowed an Air France airliner hijacked by two members of the PLO to land at Entebbe Airport. In the subsequent rescue operation, which was conducted solely by the Israelis, nearly all the hostages were freed. Humiliated by the successful Israeli raid, Amin directed that more than 200 senior officers and government officials be put to death. He also expelled foreigners from Uganda and unleashed new rounds of violence, ordering the execution of anyone suspected of opposing him.

Uganda's role in the Entebbe affair was very disturbing to many foreign governments, and the British responded by closing their Office of High

Martin H. Levinson

Commission in Kampala. To get back at the Brits, Amin awarded himself a medal, the CBE—Conqueror of the British Empire, in 1977. That same year a *Time* magazine article described the Ugandan strongman as a "killer and clown, big-hearted jester and strutting martinet."

In 1979, an invasion by Tanzanian forces caused Amin to flee to Libya, taking with him his four wives, several of his 30 mistresses, and about 20 of his children. He then went to Iraq before settling in Saudi Arabia, where the Saudis provided him with a house, a monthly stipend, domestic servants, cooks, drivers and some cars.

Amin left Uganda with an annual inflation rate of 200%, a national debt of $320 million, a wrecked agricultural sector, boarded-up factories, ruined businesses, and tens of thousands of dead bodies. None of this seemed to trouble him and he never expressed any remorse for the abuses of his regime. In 1999, Amin told a Ugandan newspaper, "I'm very happy now, much happier now than when I was president." He died content in 2003.

Robert Mugabe (1924-   )

Robert Mugabe has been the leader of Zimbabwe since 1980. Under his administration Zimbabwe has gone from being one of the most prosperous African states to a nation with the highest inflation rate in the world (in 2008, the inflation rate was officially estimated at 11 million percent). Mugabe's policies have also caused Zimbabwe to have the lowest life expectancy rate in the world—37 years for men, 34 for women. On the education front, Zimbabwe's Catholic Archbishop Pius Ncube says this about his homeland; "We had the best education in Africa and now our schools are closing."

In his youth, Mugabe was a studious lad, and over the course of his lifetime he has attained seven academic degrees. But Mugabe also possesses, as he once succinctly put it, a "degree of violence." In the early 1980s, he made clear the extent of that degree when he had more than 20,000 Ndebele civilians killed by his North Korean trained Fifth Brigade during the *Gukurahundi*—"the early rain that washes away the chaff"—ethnic massacres.

Mugabe also sanctioned violence in a land reform policy that allowed landless peasants to forcefully invade Zimbabwe's commercial farmland, driving successful farmers off their lands. This land reform policy greatly hurt Zimbabwe's ability to produce food, but it did not hurt Mugabe, as he used the banner of land reform to seize three large farms for himself. Once the "bread basket" of southern Africa and a major agricultural exporter, Zimbabwe now relies upon food programs and support from the outside to feed its population. A third of Zimbabweans depend on food supplies from the World Food Program just to avoid starvation.

In 2005, Mugabe ordered a raid on what his government termed "illegal shelters" in Harare, resulting in 10,000 poor people being left homeless from Operation *Murambatsvina* ("Operation Drive Out the Rubbish"). The authorities had moved poor people to the area in 1992, telling them not to build permanent homes, which led them to build makeshift shelters out of cardboard and wood. Mugabe's latest palace, a 25-bedroom mansion that cost more than ten million US dollars to build, is located about a mile from the destroyed shelters. (Mugabe's wife, Grace, oversaw construction of that mansion. A woman like Imelda Marcos, with expensive taste in shoes, Grace has been quoted as saying that because of her narrow feet she can "only wear Ferragamo.")

Mugabe holds a number of honorary degrees from various international universities. But not the University of Edinburgh. In June 2007, that school withdrew the honorary degree they had awarded him 15 years earlier. As a result, Mugabe holds the dubious distinction of being the first international figure ever to be stripped of an honorary degree by a British institution of higher learning. One thing you can say about the English, they really know how to hurt a guy.

POL POT (1925-1998)

Pol Pot grew up in a middle-class Cambodian household. When he was 24 he decided to go to Paris on a government scholarship to study radio electronics. There he devoted his time to radical student politics and Marxism, enlisting members to the cause from his Latin Quarter apartment. After failing his exams in three successive years, he lost his scholarship and returned to Phnom Penh in 1954.

Back home, the Polster used his ability to mix charm and grace with a stubborn ruthlessness to rapidly move up the ranks of the underground Cambodian communist party. In 1962, he became its Secretary General. The following year he was forced to flee into the bush to escape the wrath of Prince Norodom Sihanouk, leader of Cambodia. From there he waged war against the US-backed Cambodian government.

In 1975, Pol Pot came to power with the Khmer Rouge and he quickly set about transforming Cambodia into his vision of an agrarian utopia by emptying the cities; abolishing money, private property, and religion; and setting up rural collectives. His radical social experiment, derived in part from Maoist China, resulted in a death toll estimated at 1.5 million people, which translates to one in five Cambodians. (This ratio of deaths to population makes the Cambodian revolution the most murderous in a century filled with revolutions.)

Pol Pot hated people that he considered "intellectuals" and had many of them killed. Such intellectuals included individuals with college educations, civil servants from the previous regime, Buddhist monks, Muslim leaders,

Christian clergy, teachers, and virtually everyone from the middle class. Wearing glasses or knowing a foreign language was considered evidence that one was an intellectual.

The Khmer government fell in 1979 when Vietnam invaded Cambodia after a series of violent border incidents. Pol Pot and his forces once again ran into the jungle as evidence of their carnage was publicized around the globe. For those interested in films about the subject, the 1984 movie *The Killing Fields* offers a highly compelling re-creation of the immense suffering endured by the Cambodian people under Pol Pot's rule.

In August 1979, a Phnom Penh "people's revolutionary tribunal" tried Pol Pot in absentia for genocide and sentenced him to death. But, with the help of a US government that was happy to have Pol Pot fighting its enemy Vietnam, he was able to avoid being executed. He also managed to avoid having to stay with his wife who had become insane. He divorced her and in 1985 married a much younger woman, with whom he had a daughter.

In 1997, following a bloody power struggle inside the Khmer Rouge, Pol Pot was arrested by his former Khmer colleagues and charged with treason. After a "people's tribunal" sentenced him to life under house arrest, he gave an interview in which he declared, "I did not join the resistance movement to kill people, to kill the nation....My conscience is clear." He died soon thereafter of natural causes and if there's a hell went straight to it.

DONALD RUMSFELD (1932-   )

Donald Henry "Rummy" Rumsfeld is both the youngest (at 43 years old) and the oldest (at 68 years old) person ever to have held the position of US Secretary of Defense. He currently lives in a former bed-and-breakfast that was originally a plantation home called "Mount Misery." That's an exceptionally fitting place name when you consider that Rumsfeld brought a heap of despair to our nation in his management of the Iraq War.

Rumsfeld's early career involved a stint in the US Navy, a job as a Congressional administrative assistant, and work in investment banking. In 1962, at the age of 30, he ran for Congress and served there for almost four terms before going to work for the Nixon administration as Director of the US Office of Economic Opportunity. President Nixon said this about Rumsfeld: "He's a ruthless little bastard. You can be sure of that." The following paragraph shows Nixon's assessment was spot on.

As the CEO of G.D. Searle Co., Rumsfeld rammed sugar substitutes through the Food and Drug Administration's approval process, even though scientists believed the fake sugar contributed to several thousand Americans' developing brain cancer; he plotted with Dick Cheney to form a secret government-in-waiting during war games in hidden bunkers; he allowed the opium fields in post-Taliban Afghanistan to grow unchecked, resulting in millions of future heroin addicts; and he sanctioned torture at Abu Ghraib.

Rumsfeld was named Secretary of Defense soon after President George W. Bush took office in 2001, and following the September 11th attacks he led the military preparation and implementation of the US incursions into

Afghanistan and Iraq. He pushed hard to send as small a force as possible to both these conflicts, an idea that was opposed by many US military leaders and termed the Rumsfeld Doctrine. This policy proved disastrous, as there were not enough American troops to stop the looting of Baghdad or to contain a widespread insurrection in Iraq.

In December 2004, Rumsfeld received a great deal of criticism after a "townhall" meeting with US troops, where he replied to a soldier's statements about inferior military equipment by saying, "you go to war with the army you have, not the army you want." He was also heavily censured for using a signing machine rather than individually signing over 1,000 condolence letters to families of soldiers killed in Iraq and Afghanistan.

In early 2006, in a move unparalleled in modern American history, eight retired generals and admirals called for Rumsfeld to resign because of his poor military planning and strategic know-how. Many active military brass also wanted Rumsfeld to step down. President Bush responded by saying that Rumsfeld is "exactly what is needed," and defended him in his much-lampooned "decider" remark.

Rumsfeld resigned from his post on November 6, 2006. In a farewell ceremony attended by President Bush a month later, Rumsfeld's long-time political ally Vice President Dick Cheney called Rummy "the finest secretary of defense this nation has ever had." Perhaps Cheney is ignorant of the fact that some US defense secretaries have actually helped America win wars.

DICK CHENEY (1941-   )

In the 1960s, when Dick Cheney became eligible for the draft, he was a supporter of the Vietnam War. To show that support, he applied for and received five draft deferments. When asked about those deferments in 1989, Cheney said, "I had other priorities in the '60s than military service." Clearly one of those priorities was to not risk getting killed fighting for his country.

From 1978-1989, Cheney served as a congressman from Wyoming. In that position he voted against (a) the Head Start program, (b) making Dr. Martin Luther King Jr's. birthday a holiday, (c) a resolution calling on the South African government to free Nelson Mandela, and (d) the creation of a US Department of Education. (His wife later served as the head of that agency.)

Although Cheney speaks like a hawk, when he was George H.W. Bush's Secretary of Defense he cut the budget and downsized the military. He later blamed President Clinton for doing the same thing.

After Cheney left the Department of Defense he decided to serve the nation by becoming the CEO of Halliburton, one of the biggest oil-services companies in the world and an outfit that has reaped hundreds of millions of dollars from no-bid contracts in Iraq. (Internet pundit John Burnett has described Halliburton's deals as recalling a Vietnam Era controversy. He claims Vice President Cheney's ties to Halliburton are reminiscent of President Lyndon B. Johnson's relationships with Brown & Root, which is today a Halliburton subsidiary knows as Kellogg, Brown & Root; a company that Johnson steered business to.) In his first year as CEO, a job Cheney obtained with no previous business experience, Halliburton jumped from 73rd to 18th on the Pentagon's list of top contractors.

Following the September 11th attacks in 2001, Cheney declared in several public speeches that there was a connection between Al-Qaeda and Iraq, despite opposing statements from the Pentagon. This allegation drew criticism from various members of the intelligence community and several leading congressmen. Cheney blithely ignored their censure.

In 2003, the year the war in Iraq began, Cheney asserted the claim of executive privilege and refused to release required reports to the National Archives and Records Administration office charged with ensuring that the executive branch protects classified information. This led media outlets such as *Time* and *CBS News* to sarcastically advance the notion that the vice president had created a "fourth branch of government" that was above the law. Representative Harry Waxman, the chairman of the House Oversight and Government Reform Committee, described Cheney's position on this matter as "very dangerous" and "ridiculous."

On February 11, 2006, turning to shoot a quail while hunting on a southern Texas ranch, Cheney "accidentally" shot Harry Whittington, a 78-year-old Texas lawyer, in the face, neck and upper torso with birdshot pellets. He denied that alcohol had anything to do with the shooting, although he had had a beer at lunch, and did not talk to police until the next day.

On February 27, 2007, a suicide bomber killed 23 people and wounded 20 more outside Bagram Air Base in Afghanistan during a visit by Cheney. A Taliban spokesman took responsibility for the attack and said the vice president was its intended target. But the Taliban was wasting its time trying to kill Cheney—a heavy smoker who has survived four heart attacks. The man is indestructible.

KEN LAY (1942-2006)

Ken Lay was the CEO and chairman of Enron Corporation from 1986 until his resignation in January 2002. He gained lots of notoriety for his role in the corruption scandal that led to the collapse of Enron. Today, Lay and Enron have become synonymous with corporate abuse and accounting fraud.

Kenneth Lee "Ken" Lay was not born wealthy. As a youngster in Tyrone, Missouri, he earned money by delivering newspapers, mowing lawns, and doing assorted odd jobs. His father, Omer, was a Baptist preacher and part-time tractor salesman. Lay's ascendance from a small-town nobody to CEO and chairman of a multi-billion-dollar corporation is a true-life rags-to-criminal-riches tale.

In September and October 2001, Lay sold large amounts of his Enron stock as its price declined. At the same time, he encouraged Enron employees to buy more stock, telling them the company would bounce back. What he didn't tell them was that the company was going broke, that they would be locked out of accessing their investment accounts, and that he had sold more than $300 million of Enron stock from 1989 to 2001. The subsequent Enron bankruptcy cost 20,000 workers their jobs and many their pensions and dreams of a comfortable retirement after a lifetime of work. Investors too suffered—they lost billions.

As news of the scandal became more widely known, Lay claimed that he wanted to get his story out. But he went back on a promise to testify before Congress, taking the Fifth instead. He maintained Enron's collapse was due to a "conspiracy" waged by unscrupulous stock manipulators, nefarious executives and unfair journalists.

On July 7, 2004, Lay was indicted by a grand jury in Houston for his role in the Enron disaster. He was charged in a 65-page indictment with 11 counts of securities fraud, wire fraud, and making false and misleading statements. Lucky for Lay he passed away before the trial could begin.

A memorial was held a week after his death at the First United Methodist Church in Houston. It was attended by nearly 1,200 guests, including former president George H.W. Bush, who did not speak. Former Enron president and longtime Ken Lay friend Mick Seidl, who did speak, described Lay as a "straight arrow—a boy scout, if you will—who lived by Christian-Judeo principles," adding "I am saddened he will be remembered for the Enron indictment and trial…An overzealous federal prosecutor and the media have vilified a good man. It was total character assassination." Others at the service delivered similar encomiums.

On October 17, 2006, a federal court declared that since Lay had died prior to exhausting his appeals, his conviction would be abated. When abatement occurs the law views it as if the person had never been indicted, tried and convicted. But Lay did not get away with his crimes scot-free. Following the Enron collapse and allegations against him of fraud and questionable accounting practices, the name outside the Ken Lay YMCA in Cinco Ranch, Texas, was made 70% smaller.

MUAMMAR AL QADDAFI (1942-   )

On September 1, 1969, Muammar Al Qaddafi and a small group of military officers staged a coup against King Idris I, while the Libyan sovereign was at a Greek resort for medical treatment. Soon thereafter, Qaddafi was made head of the new Libyan Arab Republic. He has continued in that position for 40 years, which is quite an impressive achievement for a lad who was raised in the desert by poor nomadic parents.

When Qaddafi came to power he introduced a system that he termed *Islamic Socialism* to Libya. It emphasized ideals such as social welfare, "liberation," and education. However, in practice, Libya's political system is far from idealistic and there have been times when Qaddafi has responded to domestic and external opposition with violence (e.g., in 1980 Libyan hit squads were sent abroad to murder Libyan dissidents living in foreign countries).

During the 1970s, Qaddafi's regime was involved in subversion and terrorist activities in both Arab and non-Arab states. He reportedly bankrolled the "Black September Movement," which perpetrated the Munich massacre at the 1972 Summer Olympics. By the mid-1980s, Qaddafi was widely regarded in the West as the principal financier of international terrorism. (He was accused by the United States of masterminding and funding the 1986 Berlin discotheque bombing that killed three people and wounded more than 200.)

President Reagan labeled Qaddafi "the mad dog of the Middle East" and to get rid of him he ordered American warplanes to bomb his tent and house in Tripoli. Qaddafi survived the attack, but one of his daughters was killed.

For most of the 1990s, Libya endured economic sanctions and diplomatic isolation as a result of Qaddafi's refusal to allow the extradition to the US or UK of two Libyans accused of planting a bomb on Pan Am Flight 103, which exploded over Lockerbie, Scotland, killing 270 people.

With the coming of the new millennium, Qaddafi decided to rehabilitate Libya's image as a pariah state. In 2003, he accepted Libyan responsibility for the bombing of Pan Am Flight 103—agreeing to compensate the victims' families—and renounced terrorism. Then he gave up Libya's covert nuclear program.

In December 2007, Qaddafi was feted in Paris. A month later, Libya, a country that until 2003 was under United Nations Security Council sanctions, took over the Council's presidency. In January 2008, the Libyan foreign minister made an unofficial visit to Washington and was given a personal tour of the White House.

While Qaddafi keeps pressing for Libya's acceptance in the global community, Libya continues to operate outside international norms by jailing political prisoners, torturing detainees, and ignoring the rule of law (e.g., in August 2008, Qaddafi reacted to his son's arrest in Switzerland on a charge of servant-beating by halting all oil shipments to Switzerland, padlocking the doors of Swiss companies in Libya, and seizing two Swiss nationals as hostages). I suppose when you've been in office as long as Qaddafi has, old habits are hard to break.

OMAR AL-BASHIR (1944-   )

Omar al-Bashir, the current president of Sudan, grew up in impoverished circumstances in a small village north of Khartoum. To escape poverty he joined the army where he rose quickly through the ranks to become a general. In 1989, at the relatively young age of 45, General al-Bashir took charge of a military coup that overthrew Sudan's democratically elected prime minister.

After establishing himself as the leader of the nation, al-Bashir banned all political parties, censored the press, and disbanded Parliament. He installed himself as Chairman of the Revolutionary Command Council for National Salvation (a newly established body with legislative and executive powers over the country) and took the posts of head of state, prime minister, chief of the armed forces, and minister of defense. Power was the game and Omar al-Bashir was the name.

He subsequently allied himself with Hassan al-Turabi, leader of the National Islamic Front, and began a program to "Islamicize" the state. In 1991, al-Bashir implemented Shariah law (e.g., stoning woman to death for adultery, chopping off anatomical parts for stealing, imposing the death penalty for gay sex) in northern Sudan (a predominantly Muslim Arab area), enforcing it through Muslim judges and a newly created Public Order Police. The introduction of this new police force to impose Shariah law resulted in the arrest and detention of southerners (mostly Christian Africans) and other non-Muslims living in the north.

Al-Bashir has continued the Sudanese government's policy of conducting an all- out war against southern dissidents, who want secular democracy and self-determination in Sudan. Amnesty International estimates that a million people have died thus far in this conflict. To help fund the war, al-Bashir uses money that he receives from a consortium of foreign oil companies that do business in his country. Secure in his oil wealth, he has shrugged off UN sanctions and the loss of World Bank aid and boasted, "Sudan has entered a new stage. We have learned to rely on ourselves."

Human Rights Watch maintains that al-Bashir should be investigated for instigating and condoning crimes against humanity in Darfur, a western province of Sudan, and placed on a UN sanctions list. They specifically accuse al-Bashir of using government armed forces to loot villages and rape and murder civilians in Darfur. He has done this, they say, for the purpose of ethnic cleansing. (The UN estimates that the fighting in Darfur has left as many as 200,000 dead from violence and disease. A number of UN NGOs say the figure is much larger. In 2008, the prosecutor for the International Criminal Court at The Hague requested ten indictments against al-Bashir for genocide, crimes against humanity, and war crimes that have been committed in Darfur.)

These days, with widespread food shortages and a decimated economy, Sudan is a terrible place to live for many of its people. But al-Bashir doesn't seem to care. During a civil war in the 1990s, while he was bombing his countrymen in the south, he honored himself with a national medal to commemorate the tenth anniversary of the coup that brought him to power. Perhaps to pay tribute to his role in advancing hardship and hunger in Sudan, al-Bashir should take himself out for a good meal.

RADOVAN KARADZIC (1945-   )

In 1990, Radovan Karadzic, a no-great-shakes psychiatrist, minor poet, and white-collar criminal, helped form the Serbian Democratic Party, which was set up in response to the rise of national and Croat parties in Bosnia and dedicated to the goal of a Greater Serbia. Less than two years later, as Bosnia-Hercegovina gained recognition as an independent entity, Karadzic declared the creation of the independent Serbian Republic of Bosnia and Hercegovina, later renamed Republika Srpska, with its capital in Pale and himself as head of state and commander of 80,000 Yugoslav army troops stationed in the Republic. Under orders from Karadzic this military group, along with Bosnian-Serb militias, unleashed the dogs of war on tens of thousands of Bosnian Muslims and Bosnian Croats.

In 1995, Karadzic was jointly indicted with the Bosnian Serb military leader Ratko Mladic by the International Criminal Tribunal in The Hague for war crimes that they committed during the 1992-95 Bosnian War. Among those crimes are claims that their forces killed at least 7,500 Muslim men and boys from Srebrenica in July 1995 as part of a campaign to "terrorize and demoralize the Bosnian Muslim and Bosnian Croat population." They were also charged with the shelling of Sarajevo and the use of 284 UN peacekeepers as human shields in May and June 1995.

In 1996, Karadzic had to step down as president of the Serbian Democratic Party, as the West threatened sanctions against Republika Srpska. He later went into hiding, which helped Karadzic to avoid the fate of Serbian president Slobodan Miloseviç, who was sent to The Hague to stand trial for his war crimes.

As a man on the lam, Karadzic managed to get a novel published in 2004. Set in the 1980's, *Miraculous Chronicles of the Night*, Karadzic's fourth underground publication, was short-listed for Serbia's top literary award, the Golden Sunflower.

In May 2005, investigators reported two separate sightings of Karadzic—one allegedly with his wife Ljiljana in southeastern Bosnia, and the other with his brother Luka in Belgrade. Two years later, Reuters, citing monitored telephone conversations, reported that Karadzic was living in Russia; the Russian government denied the allegation.

In July 2008, after more than a decade on the run, during which time he gave lectures in disguise in front of hundreds of people and engaged in the practice of alternative medicine (he even had his own website), Karadzic was finally captured in a Belgrade suburb and extradited to The Hague for prosecution. His supporters, a rather large number of Serb ultranationalists for whom Karadzic is a symbol of brave resistance and a hero, say he is being singled out for punishment and that he is not guiltier than other wartime political leaders who have engaged in battle. To his loyal followers, Karadzic will always be the leader of the pack.

Mahmoud Ahmadinejad (1956-)

Mahmoud Ahmadinejad was an obscure figure when he was appointed mayor of Teheran in the spring of 2003. He was not much better known when he entered the presidential campaign two years later. However, backed by powerful conservatives who used their networks of mosques and mcshuganahs to mobilize support for him, Ahmadinejad became president of Iran on August 5, 2005, in a surprising win after gaining 62 percent of the vote in a run-off poll. (He won only 19 percent in the first round of voting but his appeal to the poor, which included wearing off-the-rack schmatas, had a significant impact in round number two.)

Ahmadinejad enjoys making controversial statements. One of his more contentious ones was that Israel should be "wiped off the map." When government leaders all over the world chastised him for this remark, Ahmadinejad responded by saying, "I am not anti-Jew, I respect them very much." That respect was called into question when he denied the existence of the Holocaust.

In December 2005, Ahmadinejad made several outrageous comments about the Holocaust, calling it "a myth" and criticizing European laws against Holocaust denial. In an interview in *Der Spiegel*, Ahmadinejad insisted there were "two opinions" about whether the Holocaust had occurred, and in an appearance at Columbia University he stated that the Holocaust should be left open to debate and research like any other historical event. Ahmadinejad has also denied that homosexuality exists in Iran.

Ahmadinejad has little patience for those who disagree with him. Human Rights Watch notes "The [Iranian] government routinely tortures and mistreats detained dissidents, including through prolonged solitary confinement…. in a pronounced shift from the policy under former president Mohammed Khatami, [Ahmadinejad] has shown no tolerance for peaceful protests and gatherings." For Ahmadinejad, it's either my way or the highway, and that road is one that frequently leads to prison.

A vocal supporter of Iran's nuclear program, Ahmadinejad has insisted that it is for peaceful purposes. He has repeatedly emphasized that building a nuclear bomb is not the policy of his government and has said that such a policy is "illegal and against our religion." But many people believe that Ahmadinejad is not telling the truth about not wanting to make nuclear arms, as there is lots of oil in Iran to meet that country's energy needs. Moreover, under the Koranic-based principle of Al Takeyya, Muslims are permitted to lie as a preventive measure against anticipated harm to one's self or fellow Muslims.

In his stands against Israel and America, and in his pursuit of atomic weapons, Ahmadinejad has become somewhat of a hero in the Arab world. And this man from Iran doesn't even speak Arabic. But that's not essential, because anyone familiar with the Middle East knows that bashing the Jews and the Great Satan in any language is usually more than sufficient to win support on the Arab street.

Osama bin Laden (1957-   )

Osama bin Laden is a militant Islamist who has been indicted in US federal court for his involvement in the 1998 American embassy bombings in Dar es Salaam, Tanzania and Nairobi, Kenya. Although bin Laden has not been indicted for the September 11, 2001 attacks, he has claimed responsibility for them. OBL is on the FBI's *Ten Most Wanted Fugitives* list.

The son of a well-connected multimillionaire Saudi construction magnate, bin Laden was raised a devout Sunni Muslim and educated in an elite secular school. He studied economics and business administration at a Saudi university and took part in the family business, the bin Laden Group. When his father died in 1968, he inherited millions. Without that vast wealth, bin Laden would have been just one more middling Middle East malcontent rather than the biggest badass barbarian in the terrorist bazaar.

In 1979, bin Laden went off to fight in the Afghan War. Nine years later he formed al-Qaeda, a radical Jihadist Arab fighting force that has been responsible for many attacks that have killed thousands of people all over the world.

Like his fellow Islamic extremists, bin Laden believes that the restoration of Shariah law will put things right in the Muslim world. He also believes that all things Western should be opposed. This latter conviction led him to issue two fatwas saying that Muslims should murder civilians and military personnel from the United States and its allied countries.

Among the mujahideen, a controversial aspect of bin Laden's ideology is that civilians, including women and children, can be killed in jihad. The reasoning behind this notion is that an innocent person who is murdered will find their correct reward in death, going to paradise if they were good Muslims and to hell if they were bad or non-believers. Not all jihadis go along with this position.

Bin Laden is more in the jihadist mainstream with his extreme anti-Jewish outlook, which involves warnings against alleged Jewish conspiracies: "These Jews are masters of usury and leaders in treachery. They will leave you nothing, either in this world or the next." He has also said that the Jews want to divide the Muslim world, enslave it, and loot all of its assets.

The US government has tried on numerous occasions to capture bin Laden or have him killed. But to date such efforts have proved unsuccessful, despite the fact that American authorities have offered a reward of $50 million for information leading to bin Laden's capture or death. (The Airline Pilots Association and the Air Transport Association have put up an additional $2 million reward.) This slippery fundamentalist desperado seems to have more lives than a cat.

KARLA HOMOLKA (1970-   )

Karla Homolka was 17 when she first met Paul Bernardo, a fellow Canadian, in a restaurant in Ontario. Later that evening they engaged in sex for several hours while their friends watched a movie in the same room. Four years after that, the two exhibitionists got formally hitched.

While they were still single, in the summer of 1990, Paul became obsessed with Tammy Homolka, Karla's 15-year-old sister. This led to a situation where, on December 23, 1990, Karla and Paul put sleeping pills in a drink Tammy was having. When Tammy became unconsciousness, Karla and Paul undressed her and Karla applied an anesthetic-soaked cloth to her sister's mouth. They then raped Tammy, who died later that evening. The official cause of her death was "accidental"—choking on vomit after consumption of alcohol.

On June 7, 1991, Karla invited 15-year-old "Jane Doe" out for a night on the town. Following some hours of shopping and dining, Karla took Jane Doe to Karla's house. There she spiked Jane's drinks with a sleeping potion. When the girl lost consciousness, Karla and her husband raped her. The next morning Jane Doe was sick and threw up, but she did not realize that she had been sexually violated. Jane Doe visited the couple again, on Dec. 22, 1992. This time the pair tried to persuade her to have sex with Paul, but she said no and left.

On June 15, 1991, Paul forced Leslie Mahaffy, a teen who was standing at the door outside her home, into his car and drove her to his house. There, Karla and Paul held the girl hostage for 24 hours while they repeatedly sexually assaulted her. They recorded the attacks on videotape, including one scene in which Karla dolls herself up for the camera before raping Leslie. The two ultimately killed Mahaffy, chopped up her corpse, encased it in cement, and dumped it in a lake.

On April 16, 1992, Paul and Karla forced 15-year-old Kristen French into their car at knifepoint. They then took her to their house, where they sexually abused and tortured the girl for three days. They subsequently murdered French and tossed her body into a ditch.

On May 5, 1993, following a police investigation, the Canadian government offered Karla a 12-year-sentence plea bargain to supply evidence on Paul's and her crimes. She accepted the pact and a week later began giving testimony to law enforcement officials.

The case attracted worldwide media attention and provoked public fury against the prosecution for cutting a deal with Karla. At the end of the trial Paul was sentenced to life in the penitentiary. Karla pleaded guilty to manslaughter and served 12 years in jail. Released from prison on July 4, 2005, she currently lives in the picturesque sun-drenched Antilles with her young son and current husband, Thierry Bordelais.